THE REASON
FOR MY HOPE

THE REASON
FOR MY HOPE
Salvation

BILLY GRAHAM

*It is either of the most least importance,
or of the most infinate importance.
The only thing it cannot be ... is moderately
important.* C.S.Lewis

W PUBLISHING GROUP

AN IMPRINT OF THOMAS NELSON

Published in Nashville, Tennessee, by W Publishing Group. W Publishing is a registered trademark of Thomas Nelson.

Thomas Nelson titles may be purchased in bulk for educational, business, fund-raising, or sales promotional use. For information, please e-mail SpecialMarkets@ThomasNelson.com.

Unless otherwise noted, Scripture quotations are taken from the New King James Version®. © 1982 by Thomas Nelson, Inc. Used by permission. All rights reserved.

Scripture quotations marked KJV are from the King James Version of the Bible.

Scripture quotations marked BBE are from The Bible in Basic English, translated by Professor Samuel H. Hooke, 1941 (NT) and 1949 (OT), and in the public domain. Published in 1965 by Cambridge University Press, Cambridge, England.

Scripture quotations marked NIV are taken from the Holy Bible, New International Version®, NIV®. © 1973, 1978, 1984, 2011 by Biblica, Inc.™ Used by permission of Zondervan. All rights reserved worldwide.

Scripture quotations marked ESV are from the English Standard Version. © 2001 by Crossway Bibles, a division of Good News Publishers.

Scripture quotations marked NLT are from Holy Bible, New Living Translation. © 1996, 2004, 2007. Used by permission of Tyndale House Publishers, Inc., Wheaton, Illinois 60189. All rights reserved.

ISBN 978-0-8499-2204-6 (IE)

Library of Congress Cataloging-in-Publication Data

Graham, Billy, 1918-
 The reason for my hope : salvation / Billy Graham.
   pages cm
 Includes bibliographical references.
 ISBN 978-0-8499-4761-2
1. Salvation--Christianity. 2. Hope--Religious aspects--Christianity. I. Title.
BT751.3.G725 2013
234'.25--dc23

2013007539

Printed in the United States of America
13 14 15 16 17 18 RRD 6 5 4 3 2 1

CONTENTS

ACKNOWLEDGMENTS

ONE OF THE GREATEST PRIVILEGES OF MY LIFE HAS been the opportunity to associate with numerous men and women throughout the years whom God has used to shape my life and sharpen my understanding of His Word, the Bible. In this book I have attempted to summarize the Good News I have preached during my ministry, and I thank God for the contribution these countless individuals have made to my life—and thus to this volume.

I am especially grateful to my son Franklin for his vision for this project and for his constant encouragement during its writing. I am very thankful also for my longtime colleague Dr. David Bruce, who gave invaluable assistance to this project by coordinating its development and publication. As they have done on previous projects, my editors at Thomas Nelson—David Moberg and Matt Baugher—have given unstintingly of their time and wisdom in this endeavor.

My special thanks to Donna Lee Toney, whose research skills enabled me to include a number of contemporary illustrations that will, I believe, make the timeless message of the Bible come alive for a new generation of readers. Of even greater importance, however, was her diligence in working closely with me to shape the manuscript into its final form. Without her dedication, unique knowledge of Scripture, and writing skills, this book would not have been possible.

—Billy Graham
Montreat, North Carolina
May 2013

INTRODUCTION

HOPE IS A GIFT. Have you ever taken hold of such a prize that leads you out of uncertainty into profound assurance? If so, you have possessed hope. When it arrives, despair departs. An old Scottish proverb says, "Were it not for hope, the heart would break." What is your heart's condition?

Mankind is barraged with news about uncertainty in the world. Hearts are paralyzed with fear about the unknown. In an article published by World Trends Research regarding our fast-paced and high-tech society, Van Wishard wrote, "The next three decades loom as the most decisive 30-year period in history."[1] Indeed, we live in tumultuous times.

Uncertainty is so widespread that the latest fad in the greeting-card industry offers encouragement through designer e-cards that pop up on user screens. One reads, "In the face of uncertainty there is nothing wrong with hope." Another card simply shows a street sign: HOPE Avenue with a placard pasted below pointing ONE WAY.

Indeed, there is only one way that leads to such certainty for today and for the future, and this is the message I want to share with you in the pages of this book. In times like these, we need a sure hope.

What is hope? Some equate it as a fanciful wish. But the word explodes with confidence to believe in something greater than ourselves, and it is not found in science, medicine, government, or technology. It is a grand gift that does not drain us of life but infuses us with lasting benefits that spring forth from its seemingly veiled treasures. If you doubt my thesis, consider these truths.

Hope is the breath of nature that surrounds us every day.

Hope is seen in a sprig that shoots up from the crevasse of a sun-dried rock, proving the water of life within.

Hope is the first ray of sunshine that peeks above the horizon—without fail—every morning with blazing truth, telling us we can make it through.

Hope is dispatched when the moon rises in the dark night, foreshadowing that a new day will dawn.

Hope swells within a sea-weary drifter when he spots a distant speck of a ship that grows larger with each passing wave.

Hope headlines commencement addresses, inspiring graduates as they embark on the new life that lies ahead, as they step out on the pathway strewn with possibilities.

Hope is the cry of a newborn baby once bound, now free.

Have you glimpsed the glow of hope? Strike a match and burn a candle. You will discover that the whisper of its flame brings life to a room, making the candle useful. Is your flame alive and making a difference in the world? You see, HOPE PIERCES THE DARKNESS.

It is the absolute assurance that there is life after death. For those who have lost loved ones—and we all have—HOPE BRINGS COMFORT to our aching souls. It perseveres, persuades, prevails.

A GIFT TO THE WORLD

For decades the world has marveled at a once crown jewel—the Hope Diamond—the dazzling, blue 45-carat gem with an estimated value of $250 million.[2] Its last owner donated the historic treasure to the Smithsonian Museum as "a gift to the world."[3] Solitary, it sits encased by thick bulletproof glass.

What hope does this rare stone bring to the peoples of the world? While it is grand in glory, it is untouchable; valuable but not priceless; a gift *to* the world but protected *from* the world, locked for safekeeping.

Is hope for you locked up, inaccessible, untouchable?

Maybe you are longing for hope and cannot find it. In these pages we will see ourselves in this pursuit of hope that brings certainty if we embrace it. You see, it is not kept from you, locked away in a museum. It is made available and comes to you as hope from above. It is not a futuristic aspiration; it is a faith builder.

A New Document

A contemporary philosopher, the late Richard Rorty, claimed that hope placed in the promise of Jesus Christ returning to earth has failed because He has not returned. This philosopher believed a new document of promise is needed for hope to exist again.[4]

My friend, there is a document of promise that has never grown old. It is new every morning.

The Bible says that Jesus Christ is the very hope that lies within. He is Earth's only hope. He came to unlock the door of your soul to bring the light of salvation into your life. "His compassions fail not. They are new every morning; great is [His] faithfulness" (Lamentations 3:22–23). This is *the reason for my hope*, found in God's *salvation*.

The psalmist said, "My flesh also will rest in hope" (Psalm 16:9). Are you resting in such a promise? Hope is an unseen commodity that pays dividends while we still live.

Hope will accompany us through our uncertain tomorrows if we will receive, by faith, the God of hope.

Don't Give Up

There is a saying, "When the world tells us to 'Give up,' hope whispers, 'Try it.'"

When the tsunami wiped out villages along the Indian Ocean, some said that all hope was gone; yet a mother, standing in the rubble, heard the whisper of hope as she held her newborn son close. That new life had come during a catastrophic earthquake and flood, in the midst of despair.[5]

Perhaps the greatest psychological, physical, and spiritual need all people have is the need for hope that builds our faith and points us beyond our problems.

We don't see the water in the rock, but nature proves it is there.

We don't see what is along our future's pathway, but we follow its lead.

The Giver of Hope

When families felt the violent grip of loss in Newtown, Connecticut, they rightly directed their cries to the Giver of hope.

The "Gift to the world" is not on display, locked away under glass in a museum. The Gift to the world came in the form of a personal Savior who paid for our freedom with His priceless life. His Spirit remains with us today, bringing salvation to all who will take hold. This hope is an anchor of the soul, both sure and steadfast.

The message of this book is *my hope* for you. And my prayer is that you will be filled with the dividends of joy and peace in believing that you can be rescued from all that hinders, bringing you into a LIVING HOPE OF SALVATION.

—Billy Graham
Montreat, North Carolina
May 2013

CHAPTER ONE

RESCUED FOR SOMETHING

Be ready always to give an answer to every man that
asketh you a reason of the hope that is in you.

—1 PETER 3:15 KJV

HAVE YOU EVER BEEN SAVED? I have.

Many years ago I was in a plane crash that could have taken my life and the lives of others on board. It was early in my ministry, and I had traveled to western Canada to speak at a conference. Back in those days much of the air travel was aboard small planes. As I settled into my seat on a Lockheed Lodestar for the final leg of my journey, the plane ascended smoothly out of Vancouver, British Columbia, in spite of a pouring rain.

While the other thirteen passengers slept, I was taking in the beauty of the Canadian Rockies until the flight attendant whispered to me that a problem had developed. The pilot had been told by a radio tower to set the plane down as soon as possible because the storm was worsening, the rain quickly turning to snow. The quandary was that all the airports in the area had been forced to shut down due to the heavy snowfall.

When the captain located an open field below, he announced that he was going to dive through a hole in the clouds. While his commanding voice was reassuring, the mood intensified when he explained that because of the snow cover he couldn't tell how the field was plowed or how the furrows were running. "I'll leave the wheels up, and we'll slide in the snow . . . but it's going to be bumpy," he warned.

Sure enough, we touched down, and the small plane bumped hard before coming to an abrupt stop. People screamed at first, but when they realized they were safe, there were tears and sighs of relief. Hope for a safe landing was realized.

We spent the night on the plane, in the middle of a farmer's field, waiting for a rescue squad that came for us with a team of horses pulling a wagon. Dawn was breaking, and the passengers were content to ride the short distance to a waiting bus.

Not all air travel mishaps end this well, with all passengers saved from disaster.

PLUNGED INTO DARK WATERS

The nation was stunned the summer of 1999, when news flashed around the world that a small plane flown by John F. Kennedy Jr. was missing. Kennedy had left New York with his wife, Carolyn, and her sister Lauren Bessette to attend a cousin's wedding at the Kennedy family compound on Cape Cod. When they didn't show up, the wedding was postponed and the hopes for celebration turned to hopelessness and despair—a tragic story that came to an end several days later when the Coast Guard pulled the three lifeless bodies out of the private plane that had plunged into the Atlantic. The cause of the crash: pilot error.

I had visited with John and Carolyn in 1996. They were an engaging young couple with endless opportunities ahead. As a small boy, John had bravely endured the horror of losing his father, the president of the United States, to an assassin's bullet. Years later he had watched his mother die a painful death from cancer. President Kennedy's son had learned how to graciously overcome the scrutiny of the public's watchful eye and the media's constant presence. He displayed the poise of a survivor in the face of ridicule or praise.

John also had a sense of adventure. His interest in aviation intrigued me because my son Franklin also loves to fly and is an accomplished pilot. To hear Franklin describe the likelihood of what happened in the cockpit of John's plane that night was chilling. When a pilot becomes disoriented in flight, survival is unlikely.

There isn't much hope for those who crash into the sea—few survive the impact. But I know someone who did.

PULLED FROM THE OCEAN

Louis (Louie) Zamperini, a former American Olympic distance runner and World War II prisoner of war (POW), has been a friend of mine for many years.

This decorated war hero was shot down in his B-24 bomber, the *Green Hornet*. He lived to tell about the 1943 crash into the Pacific Ocean, where he drifted on a life raft for forty-seven days until he was captured by the Japanese. Louie spent twenty months in a Japanese prison camp, enduring physical and mental torture. His courageous story—and ultimate victory—is told in *Unbroken*, which reached number one on the *New York Times* bestseller list and was acclaimed by *Time* magazine as the best nonfiction book of 2010.[1]

When Louie was finally rescued from the prison camp, he returned to California a hero, only to fall victim to another enemy, imprisoned again—this time by alcohol. He tells the story of his rescue from that second prison, giving hope to weary hearts who long to be saved from mental anguish, disastrous circumstances, and physical defeat.

Rescued by Portuguese Fishermen

My friend John Coale, a successful attorney in Washington, DC, experienced his own brush with death on the sea, as he would later tell my son Franklin.[2] John and his wife, attorney and television journalist Greta Van Susteren, surprised me by attending my ninetieth birthday celebration. I was with them again in 2011, when Greta covered book signings at the Billy Graham Library with former President George W. Bush and his wife, Laura.

John knows about adventure that turns perilous. He also knows the relief of a successful rescue operation. He was saved out of the icy waters off the northwest corner of Spain in 1979, the same day that China invaded Vietnam.

At the time, John was a restless attorney looking for a thrill, but he didn't know that his voyage would turn treacherous. He had been drifting around Europe, trying his hand as a blackjack counter and had become pretty good at it. But his real love was sailing. An experienced sailor since his youth, John was waiting out the choppy waters to take a voyage from the North Atlantic to the Mediterranean. Europe's coast had been pounded with hurricane-force winds all winter, so when the wind calmed as much as it probably would, John gathered his crew—his fourteen-year-old brother and his brother's friend—and climbed aboard his sailboat. The *Wolfwood*, a thirty-five-foot steel ketch, left the port of La Caruña with three adventuresome souls aboard. Despite the squally winds, John managed to hoist the four sails and rev up the engine to a speed that would get him around the northwest corner of Spain. Fifty miles off the coast, the storm intensified, and gale-force winds began raging between thirty-five and fifty-five knots. The white-knuckled crew hung on for dear life as John worked hard to keep the boat steady while eyeing the compass.

Then he heard loud cracks! He knew it was the mast. The mainsail came down on him, and then the rear sail popped. The remaining sails collapsed and wrapped around the propeller, pulling the shaft out and causing the boat to start sinking. Chaos erupted, and the boat lost power. Like a cork on the water, the *Wolfwood* floated aimlessly as the cabin filled with water.

In those days Spain had no coast guard, so the fact that the antenna snapped didn't make much of a difference. The noise was deafening, and John had to bellow, "Abandon ship!" hoping his crew—just six inches away—would hear.

John fought the gales to inflate the raft—their only exit strategy. Grabbing essentials along with his brother and friend, John hastily transferred from the sinking boat to the sophisticated life raft and pushed the imperiled boat away as the winds battered their only hope of security. The prevailing current would pull them toward Iceland, and he knew they would never survive the thousand-mile journey. They may have been in a life raft, but they were still in extreme jeopardy.

John began shooting flares, hoping his distress procedure would be seen. As the boys were complaining about the smoke from the flares, John saw hope on the horizon—a two-hundred-foot Portuguese fishing boat. He thought to himself, *Oh man, there is help up there! Thank God, now we've got a shot* [to be saved].

After enduring six to eight hours on the ocean, the approaching boat was a welcome sight. But when it drew close and John craned his neck to look twenty-five feet straight up to the deck of safety, he wondered how they would ever ascend. Someone tossed down a rope, and it whipped around like a twister. Clutching their only lifeline, they managed to pull themselves toward the side of the ship. The wave surge acted like an elevator, hoisting each of them one at a time. The fishermen grabbed hold and tossed them fifteen feet through the air into the fish hole.

Though the rescue team did not speak English, the burly fishermen showed their thrill of triumph by bear-hugging each one as though they themselves had been saved from death at sea. John couldn't help but say, "Thank You, Lord, for giving me this day." There was hope for the future after all.

Reflecting on the experience years later, John remembered,

I didn't realize that news of the dramatic rescue had reached shore long before we did. When we docked and were escorted off the ship, television cameras and reporters were everywhere. The next day the story made the front page, with the Chinese invasion of Vietnam a secondary story. I guess that's when it really hit home that we had been saved. In my experience as a defense attorney since then, not even a judge could put the scare in me after living through something like that.

I remember surviving my first brutal storm at sea a few months before this incident. I had never been so scared in my life. A little girl was on the boat, and in her French accent she yelled to me, "Johnny, isn't this beautiful?" When I looked around and saw nothing but horror, her words caused me to look beyond the pending doom and see the powerful beauty of a storm at sea. I thought, *Even this is God's gift.* The reality of the storm at sea took away my extreme fear of the pounding waves and rushing waters because it taught me that fright can be replaced with faith in the hope of overcoming fear. To be saved out of the power of the sea made me figure there's "somebody" up there looking down.

John is so right. God looks down, and every other living creature must look up to Him.

Panic at Sea

Some experience adventure in the struggle to survive while others may thrive on adventure for the thrill alone. Still others seek adventure to escape the routine of life. God gives us the taste for adventure; it is part of the DNA of the human race. An example of this is seen in the millions of vacationers who visit exotic places across the sea.

Perhaps you are among these millions. For example, did you ever wish to travel the Mediterranean Sea aboard a luxury liner? On January 13, 2012, many did: newlyweds, retirees, university graduates, sightseers, and even experienced travelers took the trip of a lifetime aboard a large cruise ship, dubbed the *Titanic* of the twenty-first century because of its first-class accommodations and luxurious amenities. But for these adventure-seekers their dream turned into a nightmare.[3]

Two hours after boarding the *Costa Concordia* off the west coast of Italy, some passengers sat down to a seven-course dinner, sipping on wine and champagne; others were entertained by magicians in theaters or by a drama on the silver screen.

But when passengers felt a jolt and the lights went out, the taste of the wine didn't calm their nerves, nor were their minds riveted to the jumbo screen. Instead, the drama of the *Titanic* that had occurred almost one hundred years earlier—on April 15, 1912—flashed in the minds of *Concordia*'s passengers. Some wondered if the cruise line was playing a Friday-the-thirteenth prank. Celine Dion's "My Heart Will Go On," the theme song of the 1997 movie *Titanic*, was playing through the speakers in one of the restaurants when the ship hit the rocks.[4]

Imagine a jolt that knocks you off course; lights are snuffed out, leaving you in sudden darkness, and the music of romance halts, giving way to eerie silence—until a voice announces all is well and assures passengers that the electrical blackout is temporary. This was the scene. Then the command was given to "remain seated,"[5] assuring passengers that there was no cause to panic. But many who were not comforted by the announcements began assessing the situation from their iPhones.[6] The data told them that the ship was listing rapidly. Hope was in peril.

Would you have remained seated? While it is important to follow instructions, there are times when our instincts tell us that conditions have changed, and if we follow reckless orders, our lives could be in danger. This is exactly what happened on the *Costa Concordia*. As the linen-draped tables began to tip, sending fine china and crystal crashing to the floor, people began screaming and running toward the doors, fleeing the restaurants, casinos, theaters, and bars. There was bedlam as men, women, and children scrambled to the decks, hoping to find the light of the moon.

People frantically searched for life vests and gripped the ship's rails in order to stay on their feet while the captain was reporting to authorities that everything was fine and that there was only "a small technical failure."[7] The truth was that the stricken vessel had already run aground.

According to port authorities, the captain continued to respond that there were no problems. Neither the ship's owner nor the Italian coast guard knew the pandemonium that was escalating as people pushed and shoved frantically through the corridors, screaming for help and guidance to the lifeboat deck. Many crew members calmly insisted that the passengers return to their cabins or remain in the lounges. Unfortunately, some did. Thankfully, most ignored the dismal and irresponsible advice. The crew had not been given orders to abandon ship, but passengers still begged the crew to launch lifeboats to save them from drowning.

FAITH IN A LIFEBOAT

In the aftermath of the disaster, some reporters scoffed at people's fears, pointing out that the *Concordia*, unlike the *Titanic*, was just a few hundred feet from shore.

While it may not be a practical comparison, one writer called the panic that occurred on the *Concordia* the "*Titanic* effect," claiming that passengers could have had "the odd idea that they were on the *Titanic*, [and] that lifeboats were their only means of salvation." They believed that if lifeboats did not come to their rescue, they were doomed—hope lost. They even may have been lulled into thinking "that it is the boats themselves, rather than human intelligence, good order, calm, and courage that are necessary to save human lives."[8]

But panic was a natural response. If you did not see the lifeboats being lowered, would you cry out for the ship's captain to save you? Passengers knew that the elderly, young children, and the disabled would be incapable of swimming even the relatively short distance, especially in the dark and the cold.

One passenger reported that her husband insisted they jump off the stricken boat, but she hesitated because she couldn't swim. He gave his life jacket to her and jumped into the water, urging her to trust him. She did and survived, but he died in the water before they could get to shore.[9]

As the story of the *Titanic* has become part of pop culture because of the blockbuster movie, it's unlikely that anyone in the past century would ever be on a sinking boat and not consider the fate of the *Titanic*. I recall as a young boy, hearing stories about *Titanic*'s catastrophe and the vows that it would never happen again. Seems modern-day cruise-goers believed them.

Gripping What Cannot Save

When three thousand two hundred souls[10] boarded the *Concordia*, they did so in the spirit of the *Titanic*—counting on a majestic voyage of leisure and awestruck beauty. One report said that there was a festive and upbeat atmosphere on deck as the ship set sail just two hours after the sun took its evening dip into the sea. But accounts from survivors were entwined with flashbacks of *Titanic*'s doom.

The *Titanic* was acclaimed as "a monument to the promise of technology." At its launch an employee of the company boldly claimed that "not even God himself could sink this ship."[11] This assumption was backed up with the fact that *Titanic* did not carry enough lifeboats for 100 percent evacuation, if one were to be necessary. When escape from the promised safety of the vessel was vital, the lifeboats that were launched off the ship were not completely filled because there were those who still believed *Titanic* could somehow be saved. During the evacuation, there were "reports of passengers refusing to get on the lifeboats, choosing instead to stay in the warmth and light of the doomed ship."[12] They didn't believe that within an hour their decision would send them to death in the icy waters.

In contrast, *Concordia* crew members reportedly "were shoving their way past passengers. One of the crew was screaming: 'I don't want to die!'" One passenger "emerging from the terror inside the ship to find himself perched on top of the slowly submerging hull" said it was "like waking up from one nightmare and stumbling into another."[13] He couldn't find a way to save himself but was grateful that someone else did.

Thirty-two did die, as opposed to the *Titanic*'s death toll of more than fifteen hundred.[14] And instead of sinking entirely like the *Titanic*, *Concordia* came to a precarious rest on its side, balanced on a rocky underwater ledge with its port side out of the water. For more than a year,[15] the lingering sight of the half-submerged ship was a reminder that while we humans may boast of our abilities and our technology, we ultimately cannot save ourselves or the trophies of our achievements.

Geraldo Rivera made this point succinctly as host of a Fox News special on this colossal tragedy at sea that sought to answer this question: How could such a calamity happen in this day and age? The documentary concluded:

> Aboard one of these massive engineering marvels it's easy to forget that the ocean is implacable. . . . No matter how sophisticated the technology or luxurious the surroundings or immense the vessel, there is nothing that overcomes human misjudgment or recklessness or cowardice.[16]

The truth of this amazing statement is precisely why God made a way for us to be saved from ourselves. Years from now people will remember the *Costa Concordia* and be determined to build an unsinkable carrier that can overcome human error, for humanity's fundamental weakness is to think we can save ourselves by getting aboard our own design with controls in hand.

Are you one of those who would rather stay on the sinking ship in the warmth and light for a few more moments of comfort as you watch an empty lifeboat drift further away to safety? Will you finally loosen your grip from what cannot save you and commit yourself to the vessel that can take you safely to shore?

As reports continued to emerge following *Concordia*'s shipwreck, I also was struck by a story that speaks about the indifference of heart. Many of the crew members did evacuate the sinking ship in sheer panic for their own lives. The passengers did not know *the way* to the lifeboats. No emergency drill had been given prior to sailing. No evacuation instructions had been communicated. Video footage documents some crew members apparently boarding the boats with no thought of saving the women, the children, and the disabled. They brushed the shoulders of the panicked passengers without answering questions or offering assistance as they ran for their lives.[17]

We hear such stories and ask, "How could this be?" Obviously they knew the way, but they refused to stop long enough to tell others the way to safety. What a sad testament to their indifference of heart. There were, however, other stories from the *Concordia* of crew, passengers, and citizens onshore who went out of their way and even risked their lives to save others: an Indian cook who helped load lifeboats despite a serious head injury that would leave him disabled; a Peruvian waitress who died because she gave her life vest to an elderly man (who survived);[18] even the ship's purser, who had helped search the decks for passengers, said, "I never lost hope of being saved." When he was finally rescued, his mother said, "To speak to him again was like being reborn."[19]

Rescue stories always lift our spirits. Perhaps the news media, in its twenty-four-hour cycle, will become more aggressive in reporting good news, because good news certainly abounds—news of men and women who are willing to risk their lives to save the lives of others.

Just four months before the *Concordia* disaster, in fact, YouTube and nearly every media outlet showed the dramatic rescue of a young man in Utah who grounded his motorcycle to avoid a collision with a BMW. When he was thrown from the bike, his body slid under the burning vehicle. Onlookers gathered, sure he was dead but wanting to recover his body. Then an unidentified woman got down on the ground and looked into the flames underneath the car. "He's alive!" she yelled.

Construction workers and bystanders on the Utah State University campus joined efforts in saving this young man's life by lifting the vehicle and pulling him from the flames. When the young man was later interviewed from his hospital bed, he told the Associated Press, "I'm just very thankful for everyone that helped me out. . . . They saved my life."[20]

May I ask, would you have refused rescue?

RESCUED FROM SOMETHING, SAVED FOR SOMETHING

Some may say, "Oh, so that's what it means to be saved!"

I have spent my life talking about this subject. After all, who doesn't want to be saved? "Search and rescue" is a term we hear almost every day, whether in the newspaper, over the Internet, or on television or radio.

We watch people being saved from automobile accidents. We hear about children being saved from drowning. We read of others being pulled out of fiery flames. We sigh with relief when military men and women save innocent lives around the world or when the National Guard rescues families from floods left in the wake of hurricanes like Katrina and Sandy. And most of us, I believe, hope that if we find ourselves in dangerous situations, there will be someone to rescue us.

What we seldom stop to realize is that when we are rescued *from* something, we are also saved *for* something. When we are rescued by someone, we are indebted to the one who has saved us from disaster, impending doom, and perhaps death itself.

It was a privilege for me to know the late president Ronald Reagan. We talked many times about his brush with death in 1981 when he survived an assassination attempt. He considered himself forever indebted to those who took bullets for him. He was candid about his own mortality and told his son Michael, "I believe God spared me for a purpose. I want you to know that I've made a decision to recommit the rest of my life, and the rest of my presidency, to God."[21]

But even if we are saved from such experiences, we will eventually find ourselves facing other threats, whether an incurable disease, a fatal accident, or something as natural as growing old and wearing out from progression of the cycle of life.

No other human being, no matter how selfless or brave, can rescue us from the certainty of death. But that doesn't mean we can't be saved, that we have no hope of rescue. It just means we need to be clear about Who really saves us. That's why I have written this book—to share what I have learned in nearly a century of living with unwavering assurance of being saved.

So what is your story? HAVE YOU EVER BEEN SAVED?

"I only say these things so that you may have salvation."
(JOHN 5:34 BBE)

CHAPTER TWO

THE GREAT
REDEMPTION

For with the LORD there is mercy,
And with Him is abundant redemption.

—PSALM 130:7

W HAT MAKES A GOOD STORY GREAT? One movie
analyst says it's *redemption*: "all great movies are stories of
redemption." He goes on to say that right and wrong choices
are embedded in such stories.[1] Film critic Roger Ebert agreed. Responding
to a fan who noted his preference for "concepts like redemption," Ebert
admitted that the films "that affect me most deeply are the ones in which
characters overcome something within themselves."[2]

While the National Football League exhibits a rough-and-tumble
exterior, its fans enjoy a good redemption story also, especially the kind
featured in "The 10 Best Redemption Stories in NFL History." This
Internet slideshow tells the stories of players and teams—some of the
biggest names in the game—who have gotten themselves in deep trouble

both on and off the field. Some have even committed grievous acts and served time in prison. Yet each has managed to make an inspiring comeback. The author says, "People often need to reach rock bottom before they turn their lives around. And each of these stories paint a picture of hope for all of us. Hope that our mistakes can be overcome."[3]

Not everyone can relate to a movie theme where good triumphs over evil or to a fallen football star who thunders back to victory. Most of us, however, know something about redemption in another form because we exchange paper currency nearly every day for something in return; currency is backed up by a redeemable value giving us assurance of its worth.

When you receive your paycheck, for example, you can redeem it for either cash or credit to your checking or savings account. This is money you've worked hard for; when payday rolls around, you expect to receive what you've earned.

But what do you do when someone hands you a gift card for your birthday or, perhaps, for no special reason? You haven't done anything to earn it, yet if left unredeemed it is worthless to you.

GIFTS NEVER REDEEMED

You might be shocked to learn that Americans are sitting on thirty billion dollars in unused gift cards—gifts never redeemed![4] Numerous laws govern the booming gift-card business, and customers are often warned to check the issuer's redemption policy. Some cards must be redeemed by an expiration date. One online store specifies that to redeem a gift card for certain items, holders "must save the Gift Card . . . to [their] account."[5] Who would think that there would be so many strings attached to redeeming a gift? Yet the industry still seems to be flourishing.

Redemption is a word filled with hope and promise and involves a giver and a receiver. A gift is based on another's sacrifice and is rarely shunned by the one to whom it is offered. Would you say "no thanks" to someone who offered you a gift? Actually some do. The choice is ours to receive it with thanks or turn our backs, rejecting the gift and the giver.

We understand the meaning of redemption—buying something of value—exchanging one thing for another. But there is always a price to pay for redemption. More valuable than any financial redemption is the hope of a redeemed life.

Redeeming a Future

The story is told of an auction that took place at a modest sheep ranch in South Africa. The farmer had lived a lonely life after the death of his wife. The son of his old age had rebelled and left home to find his fortune, ignoring his father's promise that someday all he had would belong to the son. "Consider me dead," the son told his father. He wanted no part of being a dirty shepherd.

When the old farmer died, his belongings were auctioned to neighbors and friends who had honored the old man. When the auctioneer lifted up the last item—an old framed picture—a young man stepped forward and offered a few dollars for it. A woman then stepped forward to offer considerably more. The young man was dismayed. The woman had easily outbid him.

People watched with interest as the young man approached the woman and asked why she was willing to pay a high price for a picture that could have no possible value to her. "Oh, I didn't buy it for the picture," she said, "but for the frame—it's a rare antique and has great value." When the woman saw tears in the young man's eyes, she asked why the old picture interested him.

He answered, "That is a picture of my father, the shepherd who worked this farm, and the boy with him is the son who deserted him in his old age—I am that son. The frame means nothing to me. It's what hangs inside the frame that is priceless. I rejected everything my father offered me, especially his love, but I will spend the rest of my life trying to live up to his good name."

Greatly moved, the woman took the picture from the frame and handed it to the young man. As she did, an envelope slipped out. She opened the note and read it to the young man. "If you return to me, my son, my prayers will be answered. I will not give you a dirty sheep farm; instead, I will give you the rewards of my labor. Exchange this bank draft for the sum of money that will provide for some of your needs." It was signed, "Your loving father."

The woman watched as tears streamed down the young man's face. With compassion she said, "Now go and live a life worthy of your father's name."

The young man cashed the draft, hoping to buy back some of his father's possessions from the neighbors. But when they saw his repentant heart toward his father, they redeemed his inheritance by giving him what they had purchased at the auction. They had bought for him what he could not buy for himself. The young man lived a fulfilled life on his father's farm raising sheep in the Western Cape and caring for his neighbors—proving that his father's prayers for him had not been in vain.

A PRISONER REDEEMED

The love this father had for his son and the compassion demonstrated by the woman for the young man are attributes that come from God and are often seen in redemption stories.

Our hearts are often terrorized by evil deeds that are rushed into the headlines, scrolled across television screens, or displayed as pop-ups on computer monitors.

I recently came upon a headline that mentioned ousted Panamanian dictator Manuel Noriega and was reminded of the conflict between his cruel regime and the people of Panama in the late 1980s. A redemption story that came out of that battle for freedom is still prominent on the web.

George H. W. Bush was president during this time. I know President Bush well and have seen him agonize over sending men and women into battle, into engagements of good versus evil. But just six weeks after a victory for good—the fall of the Berlin Wall—President Bush ordered Operation Just Cause, "one of the shortest armed conflicts in American military history."[6] Among its purposes was to free American citizens imprisoned by Noriega and to fight for democracy for the people of Panama.

Delta Force, an elite Special Forces detachment of the United States Army, carried out several dramatic rescues during that time. One such mission involved the redemption of an American civilian, Kurt Muse. He had been held prisoner for nine months. Night and day he expected execution.[7]

General William G. "Jerry" Boykin oversaw the operation. Boykin later would serve as mission commander for the operation in Somalia, Black Hawk Down, and in the Pentagon as deputy secretary of defense for intelligence. In his book, *Never Surrender*, he described the strategy for rescuing "Precious Cargo," the army's code name for the captive—though "Delta [Force] pinned the big guy with an affectionate nickname: Moose."[8]

Sometime after verifying the location of Muse's cell, operators swooped down on top of the prison holding the young man, blew the cell door open, and yelled, "Muse, we're here to take you home."[9]

Muse had no hope that he would be freed from bondage that day. Now he was staring into the faces of those who had come to save him— men who came in disguise, men he had never set eyes on. He hadn't invited the rescuers into his cell to discuss a possible evacuation. He did nothing to contribute to the mission, but he had to be willing to go with them. With urgency, he put his complete trust in their ability to free him.

The Delta Force operatives pulled Muse into a Little Bird chopper and took off,[10] but during escape, the helicopter caught fire and crashed.[11] Muse was in danger of being recaptured, and his rescuers were no longer in a position to save him or themselves. Providentially, a US armored vehicle located them and whisked them to safety, their freedom secured by the members of the Night Stalkers, a special operations regiment.

Some of the soldiers severely injured during Muse's rescue were taken to the US field hospital. Muse was distraught, knowing their lives were hanging in the balance because they had risked their lives to free him from captivity. He wanted to see them, but his request was denied for security reasons.

Three days later, however, Muse got the chance to gaze into the faces of the men who saved his life. He saw the wounds in their bodies. He knew they had paid a dear price for his freedom. He took each of their hands and with great emotion said, "There's no way I can ever thank you for giving me my life back." The rescuers were overcome when their "precious cargo" returned to say thank you. One of the soldiers responded, "You being here like this says it all. . . . Now go and have a good life."[12]

General Boykin wrote, "Muse stepped back and looked at them all, lying there, wounded for him" and said, "'I love you guys. I'll never forget you.'"[13] Through the years, Moose has continued to call them all and thank them for saving his life because he's never forgotten.

Why did Moose "love" those men whom he had never known until his rescue just three days before? Why would he never forget them? And why would these soldiers risk their lives for someone they had known only by name?

Moose loved those men because they were willing to sacrifice their lives, if necessary, to free him. And those men were willing to sacrifice because they were faithful to their mission. Many years later Moose is still telling the gripping story of his miraculous rescue.

Does such a story of redemption captivate you like it does me? Why do people find it so easy to believe this account when the only eyewitnesses were the prisoner and his rescuers? We accept it because the prisoner was freed and lived to tell about it. The outcome of the rescue mission is now part of history. We believe similar accounts from mighty battles down through the ages not because we were there as witnesses; we believe these stories by faith.

If you had survived such a rescue, would you ever tire of telling how you were redeemed from prison chains and given another chance to live?

THE IDEA OF REDEMPTION

Where does this idea of redemption come from? I can tell you with certainty that redemption is as old as time itself. It is a fact of history. But people still doubt.

The greatest redemption story in history is one I've shared with people around the world for more than seventy years. For me, it is the story that never grows old. Why? Because I have been redeemed.

When I was just a young man I wrestled with something within me. I knew there was a battle within my soul, something I couldn't resolve on my own. I had been taught what was right, but my spirit wanted to do something else, something I believed would make me happy. Yet I had the nagging sense that there was something more to life than satisfying myself.

This is the ongoing struggle within all of us. But where did this conflict come from?

Biblical history gives us the details. But down through the centuries people have not wanted to believe the accounts found in the pages of the Bible and have rejected truth. Human nature says, "We weren't there to witness these things for ourselves. How can we believe such a story that God created man and woman, they disobeyed God, they were tempted by Satan, they chose to believe Satan's lie over God's promise, and now all humanity must be saved from sin?"

Whether or not we believe does not change the truth of this account. The problem is that human nature doesn't exercise faith in the truth. I know because these same thoughts once troubled my own soul. When I began to question the reality of God's claims, I wrestled with doubt. *Does He care about me? If so, why am I in conflict?*

As a teenager, I was invited to hear a traveling preacher. The advertisements called him a "fighting preacher." I liked a good scrap, so I went. The preacher was a giant of a man. Halfway through his message that night, he pointed in my direction and shouted, "Young man, you are a sinner!"

There were other guys around me, but I was convinced he had singled me out, so I ducked. But then the idea that someone would call me a sinner stirred up my fighting spirit. I told myself, "I live a good, clean, healthy, moral life. I even belong to a church." Yet I found myself in great conflict and could not resolve my own guilt over wanting to experience thrills, happiness, and pleasure in my own way. I knew I was living beneath God's standard. In God's eyes I was no different from anyone else. I wasn't a murderer. I wasn't a thief. But I was a sinner.

How did I know I fell short of God's standard? Because God puts within each soul a longing to know Him. But sin is a barrier that keeps us from enjoying a relationship with God. Sin is like a prison cell we cannot break out of. We are bound *by* it unless we are freed *from* it.

REDEEMING THE SOUL

This is the story of the first man and woman—who, by the way, were parentless. Their heritage was directly from God's perfect creation, and He gave them each a soul. He made the soul for a purpose—to experience the joy of a relationship with God that would last forever.

The Bible tells us: "And the LORD God formed man of the dust of the ground, and breathed into his nostrils the breath of life; and man became a living soul" (Genesis 2:7 KJV).

Notice it doesn't say that man became a body or man became a brain. Man certainly was created with both, but he was not a living creature until God breathed into him the breath of life, making him a living soul.

You may ask, "Just what is the soul?" The soul is the real you, the real me—the very breath of life that comes from God. The Bible says,

But there is a spirit in man,
And the breath of the Almighty gives him understanding.

(JOB 32:8)

The body is the house, the soul is the tenant, and every soul is precious to God. Jesus said that one soul is worth more than the whole world (Matthew 16:26).

God is the soul's Creator, and He holds in His hand "the breath of all mankind" (Job 12:10). Jesus is the soul's Savior: "But God will redeem my soul from the power of the grave" (Psalm 49:15). And the Spirit of God is the soul's guiding light: "The Spirit of truth . . . will guide you" (John 16:13).

Medical science has probed the intricate organs and tissues of the human body after death, but it cannot probe the soul, for it is unseen and lives eternally. The soul—the spirit of man—never dies. The Bible says, "For the things which are seen are temporary, but the things which are not seen are eternal" (2 Corinthians 4:18).

Adam and Eve, the first man and woman, were made in God's image and placed in a perfect environment. Instead of enjoying life in the garden of Eden, where they could love one another and communicate with God, they willingly chose to do the one and only thing God had forbidden them to do—eat from the Tree of Knowledge of Good and Evil. Because of God's love, He protected them from the knowledge of evil and granted them freedom to enjoy the bounty of the garden— except from one tree.

Glorious life in the garden was interrupted by an intruder. Satan, the great deceiver, presented himself in the form of a serpent and told Eve that God was withholding from them His very best. Satan, through his craftiness, tempted Eve, persuading her that she would become like God if she ate the fruit of the forbidden tree. That sounded good to Eve, so she convinced Adam, and together they exchanged a life of bliss for a life of burden.

Their sin was not that Satan tempted them; the sin was that they believed Satan's lie and then acted on it instead of believing God's Word and then obeying it. Since that time, every human has plunged headlong into Satan's trap that leads to sin. This original sin has been passed on from generation to generation, down to the present day.

Now you may say, "Well, that's not fair. Why should we pay for something Adam and Eve did?" When original sin entered the bloodstream of the human race, it blackened every soul. "Sin entered the world through one man, and death through sin, and in this way death came to all people, because all sinned" (Romans 5:12 NIV).

The sin nature has been transmitted from parent to child, and onto it we heap sins of our choosing that flow from the carnal nature that reigns within.

If we were to claim that is not true, how could we possibly explain why as children we disobeyed our parents? Why is it that our children disobey us? And if we live to see our children marry and have children, this cycle will be repeated. We know this is a fact. Why do we disobey? My friend, the Bible says that

> The heart is deceitful above all things,
> And desperately wicked;
> Who can know it?
> I, the LORD, search the heart,
> I test the mind,
> Even to give every man according to his ways.
>
> (JEREMIAH 17:9–10)

REDEEMING THE TRUTH

When Adam and Eve turned their hearts away from God in disobedience, they set their desires on Satan's deceitful ways. Their relationship with

God was marred by sin, and they fell into Satan's trap—right where he wanted them. That's when the fall of man occurred.

The first step toward sin is *listening* to Satan's lies, and that often is followed by doing what Satan tells us will bring happiness. Adam's and Eve's eyes were opened, and their sin lay bare. Instead of enjoying the status Satan promised—that they would be like God—they fell from God's favor. They were under Satan's spell, for it was this very sin—to be greater than God—that caused Satan to fall from Heaven.

Adam and Eve quickly discovered that they had made a deadly transaction, exchanging God's perfect standard for Satan's lowest blow. God had handed them a gift—Paradise—and they had turned their backs both on the gift and the Giver.

Some say, "If God really cared about Adam and Eve, He should have intervened and given them a second warning." Knowing our own hearts as we do, is it really believable that another warning would have made the difference? God knows our hearts better than we do.

REDEMPTION SHUNNED

A young couple took their children to a park one day to play. Another parent alerted them to poison ivy growing in the bushes some distance away. The young couple warned their children to stay away from the area.

Where do you think the children ran when their parents were not looking? Right into the ivy.

The father ran and caught the youngest one before she could touch it. To the father's surprise, the child jerked away from his grip. In defiance, she embraced the leaves, looked up into her father's sad face, and said, "Look, Daddy, pretty red flowers."

In spite of our children's disobedience, we do everything we can to alleviate the pain and discomfort of the consequences that result from defiance. But we cannot take away the results of disobedience. If this father could have taken the festering rash from his child, he would have, but it was not possible. Instead, with loving hands he covers her skin with medicine that will bring healing, hoping she will learn that disobedience drags behind it severe consequences.

This is the picture we see of humanity defiantly looking into the face of God and God's loving response.

Adam and Eve ignored God's warning when He said, "Of every tree of the garden you may freely eat; but of the tree of the knowledge of good and evil you shall not eat, for in the day that you eat of it you shall surely die" (Genesis 2:16–17). They didn't truly believe God's warning that if they disobeyed they would die. But sure enough, from the moment they ate of the tree, sin ravaged their souls and the dying process began, for "the soul who sins shall die" (Ezekiel 18:20).

Death was not part of God's plan for Adam and Eve. He did not intend for them to be imprisoned by sin. He gave them life. He gave them freedom in Paradise. God allowed them to walk with Him in the garden. He created them for His own pleasure. Instead the man and the woman surrendered to Satan's enticement. They chose to step out of God's will and God's perfect garden and into self-will—Satan's paralyzing grip.

I heard a man on television say, "I only have one problem in life—temptation." Temptation does entice. We are quick to grab hold of what appeals to our senses without considering the penalty for our choices that are costly and sometimes deadly. And Satan uses every deceptive trick to tantalize. He starts with a little truth but distorts its very meaning. First we look and admire, then we touch and consider, then we taste. Eventually the sweetness turns bitter.

Down through the centuries, Satan's formula has not changed. He is still up to the same cunning tricks, pulling men and women down to substandard—the devil's playground. (Why can't we learn that if we play with fire we're going to get burned?) There are two ingredients to deceit: a good bit of truth and a few little lies.

REDEMPTION—GOD'S PLAN

Many people claim they don't believe in original sin, but the story of Adam and Eve reveals the wickedness of the human heart that turns its back on God.

Late-night television uses skits to spoof the idea of sin. Animators fill the Internet with crass characterizations of Adam and Eve, quoting Bible verses and making jokes about disobedience to God. The world may laugh at the idea of sin and make jokes, but Adam and Eve did not find the curse of sin humorous. God is not laughing and neither should we, because those who jest about sin are not excused from the consequences of sin. Eventually we all find ourselves staring into the face of truth. The Bible says that man's soul is "full of troubles" (Psalm 88:3), filled with bitterness, grief, pain, and guilt.

Adam and Eve paid a price for their disobedience. They were driven out of the Paradise of God, His very presence, into the world they had chosen—a world where God's enemy, Satan, "works in the sons of disobedience" (Ephesians 2:2).

But that is not the whole story. Genesis portrays not only the beginning of the human race, but the start of God's redemptive work in history. The salvation of the human race was put in place at the very beginning. Because God so loved His creation He initiated a way to make amends for man's sin. This is the greatest search-and-rescue mission ever carried out—redemption of those made in God's image.

REDEMPTION COMES INTO VIEW

In the greatest story ever told we see this remarkable hope.

> As through one man's offense judgment came to all men, resulting in condemnation, even so through one Man's righteous act the free gift came to all men. . . . For as by one man's disobedience many were made

sinners, so also by one Man's obedience many will be made righteous. (Romans 5:18–19)

The love and mercy that overflowed from the heart of God would someday flow in the crimson blood of His Son. From the heart of God to the cross of Christ, redemption came into view. God was not willing to turn His back on the human race. His love was too deep, His mercy too wide. He longed to recover, redeem, and bring us back to Himself. "For God so loved the world that he gave his one and only Son, that whoever believes in him shall not perish but have eternal life" (John 3:16 NIV).

This is what God did for us. God took Heaven's best—the Lord Jesus Christ—to redeem earth's worst. The Son of God died on a cross, an instrument of Roman torture made for the vilest offenders.

We, as a race, have been enticed into the service of Satan, but our unfaithfulness and waywardness have not canceled out God's love for us. Instead, He has made the way for our rescue through His Son, Jesus Christ. He made the sacrifice and paid a price unthinkably greater than our true value. We are redeemed, recovered, and restored, not with money—silver and gold—but with the precious blood of Christ.

You may not believe in Satan and his vise grip on the human race, but it is brutally real, just as real as the overpowering love of God. I can testify to this. I came to believe by faith that God's redemption plan conquers Satan's entrenched wickedness that seeks refuge in our souls. God's forgiveness of sin overcomes Satan's contempt for God's redeeming love. God's forgiveness has the power to cleanse us and restore the relationship He longs to have with us. This is why He has provided the way of salvation. This is why the Bible says we "must be born again" (John 3:7).

It took me a while to grasp this great and wonderful truth. As a young man, my head resisted what my soul longed for—peace from an inner conflict. I fell miserably short of God's standard of goodness. I wanted to make my own decisions, never considering that some of my choices altered the happiness I desired.

God was not going to force His way on me. I could receive Him and live according to His high standard, or I could reject Him and live in a lowly state with Satan snapping at my heels. How could I resolve this bitterness of soul? The answer came when I considered the Bible's great redemption story. I came to the place of repentance for my sin against God, believing in what He had done for me. In order to know the peace that comes *from* God, I had to confess my sin and come *to* God.

When I went back to hear that fiery preacher, I realized he was not fighting against me. He was fighting *for* me—for my soul and the souls of everyone there. When he talked about sin, he shouted with *passion*, but when he talked about the sinner, he spoke with *compassion*.

On the night of November 1, 1934, my hardened soul was redeemed. I exchanged my will for God's way. I traded my calloused heart for a cleansed soul.

I had sought thrills. I found them in Christ.

I had looked for something that would bring perfect joy and happiness. I found it in Christ.

I had looked for something that would bring pleasure and would satisfy the deepest longing of my heart. I found it in Christ.

I had been redeemed and knew firsthand the promise of the Bible:

> In Your presence is fullness of joy;
> At Your right hand are pleasures forevermore.
>
> (PSALM 16:11)

REDEMPTION—THE GREAT STORY

God says to the human race, "I made you, and you are Mine. I have redeemed you. Return to Me" (Isaiah 43:1 and Joel 2:12, author's paraphrase). God's gift of redemption says, "I will buy you back with My blood because I love you. I will free you from the chains of sin. I will settle the conflict within and give peace to your soul. But you must come to Me with a repentant heart. You must be willing to be redeemed. You must exchange your sin-blackened heart for a new heart that is cleansed by My blood."

Redemption is the Bible's great theme.

God's redemption plan is what turned a sordid story into a great story. His rescue mission was executed through His Son, the Lord Jesus Christ, the Savior of the world. He completed His mission more than two thousand years ago, when He hung on the cross and shed His blood in ransom for the souls of mankind. He died for your sin and my sin. When He conquered death and was raised from the grave that could not hold Him in bondage, He reached out His nail-scarred hands and said, "I've come to free you from your bondage and give you new life."

This story is great because God gives each of us the choice to accept His forgiveness and live with Him eternally. The Bible says that "God is not the God of the dead, but of the living" (Matthew 22:32). God is alive and well and wants no less for those He loves.

From the cross Jesus offered each soul a gift that will last eternally—with no expiration date. His precious blood was applied to your sin. He put His life on the line for you, and His blood is credited to your account. He has covered your sin with His blood, which takes the sting of sin away.

Will you receive it? Have you read His redemption plan? It's written in blood with you in mind. Have you reached out to accept it? You cannot buy it with money; it has already been purchased for you. But you must surrender all you are hanging on to for something far better—the redemption of your soul. "After you heard the word of truth, the gospel of your salvation . . . having believed, you were sealed with the Holy Spirit of promise, who is the guarantee of our inheritance until the redemption of the purchased possession" (Ephesians 1:13–14).

Perhaps you think your life is going great and you'll wait until you are in need of rescue. When the young motorcyclist mentioned in chapter 1 climbed on his bike, he never dreamed that minutes later he would be pinned under a car in the midst of fiery flames.

We live in an uncertain world. None of us knows when our time on earth will be over. Don't take for granted the gift that God offers you. Don't presume upon His favor. Jesus has bought back our inheritance of eternal life. None of us deserves it—but He stands patiently with His hand outstretched.

When Jesus walked among men, many believed He had come to save them, but they lost all hope when He was taken down from the cross and buried in a tomb. His followers hid in disgrace and despair. Their Savior had died and left them alone. They were despondent that He had not done what He had promised—saved them from their enemies. They considered all that He had claimed and saw only the blaze of defeat. How could their Rescuer save them if He couldn't save Himself?

But the Special Force that had come down had not yet completed His mission. His followers had forgotten what He had told them: "I will come again" (John 14:3).

Redemption was fulfilled, as promised, on the third day when He rose from the grave. His resurrection conquered the enemy of death, and shortly afterward, Jesus appeared to His dejected followers who had lost faith. They looked at Jesus, the Man who had shed His blood to put to death the curse of sin. He had returned to them in all of His glory. He had won the victory over death and over sin that entangled humanity.

FROM CAPTIVITY TO REDEMPTION

When Jesus revealed Himself as the resurrected Christ that day, all barriers came down. He came into the disciples' presence and offered up His wounds as proof that He had been faithful to His mission—to "preach the gospel" and to "proclaim liberty to the captives" (Luke 4:18). It is His message for people of every generation and of every race and of every nation. Look at Jesus. He came down for you. There is an Operation Just Cause in the Bible that says:

Hear a just cause, O LORD. . . .
Save those who trust in You.

(PSALM 17:1, 7)

And He will. You are His precious cargo. He stands ready to break through the conflict that keeps you in bondage. Will you take His hand and let Him free you from the chains of sin?

Look at Jesus. Consider the wounds He endured when He died on the cross for you. It wasn't the frame of the wooden cross that had value; it was the bloodstain on the cross that was priceless. Will you repent? Will you say, "Thank You, Lord, for redeeming me"?

Don't run and hide or cover yourself in earthly pleasures that will not satisfy. Don't block out your deeper need to know God.

I have never known anyone to accept Christ's redemption and later regret it.

WHAT IS YOUR REDEMPTION STORY?

After you heard the word of truth, the gospel of your salvation . . . having believed, you were sealed with the Holy Spirit of promise, who is the guarantee of our inheritance until the redemption of the purchased possession.

(EPHESIANS 1:13–14)

CHAPTER THREE

SIN IS IN

Where sin abounded, grace abounded much more.

—ROMANS 5:20

HAS THE 'NOTION OF SIN' BEEN LOST?" You may think this question would come from a preacher like me, but the question found its way not long ago into a *USA Today* headline. In the story that followed, the reporter asked, then answered another question: "Is sin dead? No, not by a long shot."[1]

A researcher who was quoted in the article said that while many Americans do believe in sin, they tend to think, "I have to do what's best for me; I am not as sinful as most."[2]

Sounds a little like Adam, when the Lord confronted him in the garden:

"Have you eaten from the tree of which I commanded you that you should not eat?"

Then the man said, "The woman whom You gave to be with me, she gave me of the tree, and I ate."

And the LORD God said to the woman [Eve], "What is this you have done?"

The woman said, "The serpent deceived me, and I ate." (Genesis 3:11–13)

Adam blamed God for giving him the woman and then blamed Eve for giving him the forbidden fruit of the tree. Adam presented himself blameless—but he didn't fool God. Eve didn't blame herself for defying God either; she blamed the serpent for tempting her. But refusal to take responsibility for their disobedience eventually opened Adam's and Eve's eyes to the shameful reality of sin.

Many people believe that the subject of sin is only spoken about from a church pulpit. Others may think in terms of a seminary student on spring break, preaching at the beach or on a street corner, as I did many years ago when I was a Bible student. But there is great curiosity about the subject of sin from people of all persuasions.

SIN IS IN

The *USA Today* reporter asked several people to describe sin. One young man said, "You know what sin is when you get a feeling in your gut that something's wrong."[3] In a blogged response to the article, another person said he always felt dirty using foul language but didn't think it would send him to Hell.

Four-letter words have always been considered vile. But it is my belief that the most awful word known to man is *sin* because it gathers up all the wickedness mankind expresses. Three little letters make up three little words, but their message packs a powerful blow—Sin Is iN! "What is it in?" you may ask.

The answer: "You, me, and everyone who has ever lived."

Sin manifests itself in people's hearts. Self-interest lives in us, and it is at the very center of what prevents us from obeying God and keeps us distant from the God who loves us. Sin casts a searchlight on the sinner. When we see the little *i* cradled in the middle of this word, *sin*, we are looking at the guilty party. Men, women, and children need to be told that they are sinners. This is not my message. This is God's message. We can call sin a mistake, an error, or a psychological twist, but God calls it sin.

We have already seen the account of original sin. Its flame has burst into a consuming inferno because people around the world continue to heap transgressions against God. The unending conflict in the Middle East goes back in history to Abraham and his descendants and has metamorphosed into unprecedented terror today—it's called sin.

The unrest across Africa stems from hostilities of the racial divide—it's called sin.

The unparalleled power of drug cartels throughout Central and South America is burning the brains of young and old alike—it's called sin.

The ugliness of ethnic cleansing has ripped open the belly of Eastern Europe—it's called sin.

The ultramodern nations of the West have defied God's moral code of conduct—it's called sin.

Unbearable results of sinful nations seem to be pouring down upon us like an avalanche of refuse.

Sin is a fountain of woe, the mother of sorrows—as universal as human nature and as eternal as human history. Sin has caused all the war, hatred, violence, grief, and pain. Sin is our worst enemy. And it was sin that nailed the Son of God to the cross.

All the distress, bitterness, heartache, shame, and tragedy can be summed up in that three-letter word. Its meaning has an impact on every soul and overflows the boundaries of the human heart. Even death, the final enemy, has its roots in sin.

The world's system claims that the notion of sin is old-fashioned and out of date. People "in" the world prove that claim erroneous. A sociologist quoted in the *USA Today* article admitted, "Secular people still believe there's sin, judgment and punishment."[4] Sin is definitely in—in every single heart that beats.

Atheists, churchgoers, and members of various sects admit to sinning while many who claim to preach the Gospel of the Lord Jesus Christ are rebranding the idea of sin to make it more palatable. One popular television pastor said, "I never thought about (using the word 'sinners'). . . . Most people already know what they're doing wrong."[5]

That may be true, but do they know there is a penalty to be paid for "doing wrong"?

POISONOUS PRANK

Many years ago a distinguished Methodist minister was preaching on sin. Some deacons approached him afterward and said, "We don't want you to talk so plainly about sin; if you do, our people will more easily become sinners. Call their sins mistakes if you will, but do not call their mistakes sin."

The minister picked up a small bottle and showed it to the group of deacons. The bottle was clearly marked Poison.

"Would you like me to change the label?" the minister asked. "I can mark that this strychnine is the essence of peppermint to make you feel better, but if you take it you will still die. Don't you see that the milder you make the label, the more dangerous you make the poison?"

Talking about sin does not make someone a sinner. The truth is that every last one of us is born in sin, and while some may not think of themselves as sinners, God does. He hears every word we utter and knows the deepest secrets we lock away in the vaults of our hearts. The Bible says that God "knows the secrets of the heart" (Psalm 44:21). But He loves sinners more than we love sin. And that is why He sacrificed His only Son to pay the penalty for mankind's sin, which is death. It was the ultimate sacrifice—the righteous blood that flowed from the veins of the Savior of the world.

No love is greater than that.

A Popular Topic: Sin

Modern technology has penetrated some of the most complex codes embedded in electronic brains, retrieving from highly sophisticated and secured computers what was never intended to be discovered. I have never learned to use a computer, but I am surrounded by family, friends, and colleagues who have mastered many forms of technology that I find fascinating and can be used for good causes. But technology can also entrap. "Be sure your sin will find you out" (Numbers 32:23) is being proven constantly.

A recent Internet article detailed fifteen criminal cases that had been solved with digital evidence.[6] GPS tracking devices can locate adulterous husbands, unfaithful wives, and wayward teenagers. Cell phones can pinpoint the place a person denied going to, but they can also discover an abducted child.

I have always been a newshound and have appreciated communication in its many forms. Today millions of people communicate through the keyboard, and their innermost thoughts ride the airwaves. Sadly, it seems many find it easier to pour out their emotions as long as the computer screen is all that is looking back. Blogs and social media offer millions the platform to weigh in on anything and everything.

I was told of an interesting online exchange between men and women from around the world. An Australian blogger on an air-travel forum sent out a question about sin to whoever would log in, read, and then respond:

> Last night, I watched [the television show *A Current Affair*] in Australia. The reporter asked lots of people about sin. The reporter asked "What does sin mean? Do you have sin?" Then most people who were interviewed laughed so loudly!! I was surprised and wondering why they laughed when they heard the word "SIN"???
>
> Do you think that sin is funny?

A Canadian answered, "Define 'sin', and then we'll talk."

Someone from the United States chimed in: "Definition of sin: Falling short of perfection as defined by GOD."

An Englishman responded, "No. Falling short of perfection as defined by humans trying to interpret what God wants."

Someone from Ireland said, "Humans have been conditioned to believe that they must follow a set of rules, that govern the way they live."

Another Australian submitted his thought saying, "I think the term [sin] is considered irrelevant or silly."[7]

While this discussion certainly reflects a variety of answers, it also reveals the singular fact that the human race is acutely aware of its sinful nature but doesn't fully comprehend its devastating results. Individuals are responsible for their sins, but we do not determine what they are. We need the Bible for that. So what does it tell us about this very popular subject that weighs down every man, woman, and child?

SIN DEFINED

Sin is the transgression of the law of God (1 John 3:4). The Bible says that whoever breaks one law is guilty of breaking all of them (James 2:10). Sin is an intrusion into a forbidden area—an overstepping of the divine boundary between good and evil. The Bible classifies us all as sinners and says that all are under sin (Galatians 3:22).

Iniquity is another word for *sin*. Iniquity refers to our corrupt nature, from the inside out. "Every inclination of the human heart is evil from childhood" (Genesis 8:21 NIV). And Jesus said, "For out of the heart come evil thoughts—murder, adultery, sexual immorality, theft, false testimony, slander" (Matthew 15:19 NIV).

Sin is also described as a trespass—unlawfully going where we shouldn't. It is feeding selfishness instead of submitting to divine authority. The Bible says that we "were dead in trespasses and sins . . . and were by nature children of wrath" (Ephesians 2:1, 3). Instead of making God the center of our lives, we make self the center of our lives. Our supreme motive and supreme rule is putting self in God's place. This is what happened with Satan. This is what happened with Adam and Eve and everyone who has lived since. We trespass against God when we depend on self-sufficiency instead of practicing faith in God, self-will instead of submission to God, and self-seeking instead of serving God.

Sin is lawlessness as well. This means a spiritual anarchy or rebellion against God (Deuteronomy 9:7). David, the great king of Israel confessed,

> Against You, You only, have I sinned,
> And done this evil in Your sight.
>
> (PSALM 51:4)

Sin is unbelief, an insult to the truthfulness of God. It is unbelief that shuts the door to Heaven and opens the door to Hell. It is unbelief that rejects the Word of God and refuses Christ as Savior. It is unbelief that causes people to turn a deaf ear to the Gospel and to reject the miracles of Christ. And it is unbelief that causes us to turn a blind eye to our own sin: "If we say that we have no sin, we deceive ourselves, and the truth is not in us" (1 John 1:8).

Sin is of the devil. "The one who does what is sinful is of the devil, because the devil has been sinning from the beginning" (1 John 3:8 NIV). All wrongdoing is sin. To sum it all up—God hates sin (Psalm 5:5).

WHAT IS A SINNER TO DO?

Sin incurs the penalty of death, and no one has the ability to save himself from sin's penalty, nor to cleanse his heart of its filth. Jesus said, "Whoever commits sin is a slave of sin" (John 8:34). That's the bad news. Now here is the Good News: *God loves the sinner*, but He demands repentance. No one from the online conversation discussing sin seemed to know sin's remedy, yet it was God's love for sinners that sent Jesus down from Heaven to wipe out the very thing that holds us hostage to guilt, shame, and utter hopelessness. He has crushed sin's power through His love, which reflects His compassion, mercy, and divine grace. The Bible says,

Who is a God like You,
Pardoning iniquity
And passing over the transgression of the remnant of His heritage?

He does not retain His anger forever,
Because He delights in mercy. . . .

You will cast all our sins
Into the depths of the sea.

(MICAH 7:18–19)

God's offer is to all sinners, "I will cleanse them from all their iniquity by which they have sinned against Me, and I will pardon all their iniquities" (Jeremiah 33:8). Sin's masterpiece of hopelessness is overshadowed by God's masterpiece of forgiveness and mercy.

Humanity's chief trouble is sin. God's chief truth is the wonderful gift of His salvation. And Jesus Christ is the only remedy for sin. "If we confess our sins, He is faithful and just to forgive us our sins and to cleanse us from all unrighteousness" (1 John 1:9).

The Bible declares, "All unrighteousness is sin" (1 John 5:17). *All* is an important word. It encompasses not only *all* people but *all* actions, words, unspoken thoughts, and attitudes. Even when directed at others, these things are just as harmful to us. Anger toward others never relieves our hearts. Jealousy causes some to outwardly rage while others see the inwardly. Gossip poisons our tongues and preys on our minds. Sin violates the very love of God and breaks the law of God set forth to protect us from these hateful and harmful dispositions. This is the picture of unrighteousness. The Bible says, "For all have sinned and fall short of the glory of God" (Romans 3:23). We can pretend that we are not unrighteous, but in our hearts we know we are.

Who Cares About the Law Anyway?

Perhaps you say, "Society has become sophisticated. We don't need God's law to rule us." Are you among those who would like to abandon all law?

Would you like to get out on the roadways of the world and drive a vehicle with no signposts, no speed limits, no rights-of-way, and no stoplights to keep others from crashing into you?

Do you think planes could successfully take to the friendly skies without air traffic control?

Would you like to undergo surgery with the scalpel in the hand of someone who had never passed Biology 101 or graduated from medical school?

Would you enjoy sports without rules or boundaries? What would be the point? When a player on the field or court goes out of bounds, he has committed a transgression, and there is a penalty for that transgression. This is common sports language. We accept the rules; in fact, we love them. If we are rooting for our team and the other team commits a transgression, we cheer.

Do you begin to see what is in our hearts? Do you think the Lord cheers when we go out of bounds? No, His heart is grieved. The Bible says, "Every intent of the thoughts of [man's] heart was only evil continually. And the Lord was . . . grieved in His heart" (Genesis 6:5–6). God's desire is for man to be victorious over sin.

Satan, on the other hand, is doing all he can to cause us to fail, to destroy us. Scripture tells us that our "enemy the devil prowls around like a roaring lion looking for someone to devour. Resist him" (1 Peter 5:8–9 NIV).

Rules of the game are necessary, even welcome. Laws are necessary, and we should be thankful for them. But instead of honoring the law, we corrupt the laws that govern day-to-day living. We also corrupt the law of God. His commands are designed for our good, to show us where we fall short.

God's law proves that we do not measure up. When we violate His perfect law, sin overtakes us. Sin is stepping over a boundary that God put in place. When we step over the threshold, we transgress against Him.

I would tell the commenters on the airline forum that we do not define sin. God defines it clearly in His Word and has shown us the right way to live. We're not talking about a list of dos and don'ts. God's commands are designed to show us His goodness and His desire for us to live a better way than what we would choose for ourselves.

Scripture says, "The law is holy, and the commandment holy and just and good" (Romans 7:12). God wants us to stay within the boundaries He set so that we can have victory over sin.

Why? Once again, because God loves sinners.

CAN SIN BE OVERTURNED?

The word *sin* appears in the first book of the Bible and shows sin's power over mankind: "If you do not do what is right, sin is crouching at your door; it desires to have you, but you must rule over it" (Genesis 4:7 NIV). Sin has been crouching at humanity's door ever since then.

The first time sin is mentioned in the New Testament, it shows its vulnerability to the power of the Redeemer. The angel told Joseph, "[Mary] will give birth to a son, and you are to give him the name Jesus, because he will save his people from their sins" (Matthew 1:21 NIV).

Jesus said, "For I did not come to call the righteous, but sinners, to repentance" (Matthew 9:13).

Why did Jesus say that He would not call the righteous? Because the Bible says, "There is none righteous, no, not one" (Romans 3:10).

I wish I could speak to each one who participated in the online forum about sin. I would tell them first that God loves them, just as He loves each one reading the pages of this book. It shows that you are interested in the things of God. His desire is to lift us out of sin and set our feet on a new path.

Some may think sin is funny, but the Bible describes the pain that sin brings:

> My guilt has overwhelmed me
>> like a burden too heavy to bear. . . .
> because of my sinful folly.

> (PSALM 38:4–5 NIV)

That doesn't sound like sin is too funny, does it? Sin is a serious matter!

CAN YOU BE REMADE?

We've seen that sin means doing anything that is against the holy character of God, that sin is built into our very nature, that sin leads to death, but God has redeemed us from sin. This is why the Bible says we must repent of our sins and submit to God. We must become clay in His hands so that He can mold us into His likeness.

Why would anyone resist the touch of the Master's hand that brings hope for a meaningful life in Jesus Christ? I've heard many tell about a sculpture artist who was chipping away at a chunk of stone.

A man asked him, "What are you doing?"

The artist replied, "I am sculpting an elephant."

The man asked, "How do you know what to chip away?"

The sculptor smiled and said, "I chip away anything that doesn't look like an elephant."

This is what God wants to do with our lives. We were made in His image, but sin distorted everything about us—our bodies, our hearts, and our minds. When we submit to Him and place our lives in His care, He will chip away at whatever keeps us apart from Him so that we can wholly be part of Him.

You see, God doesn't just rescue us from the bondage of sin. He doesn't just redeem us. When He saves us, the Holy Spirit begins a transformation in us. He forgives the curse of sin against us and remakes us to live for Him.

Some claim that they don't know what sin really is. I am convinced that no one will think right, act right, or be right until we get the right idea of sin. Perverted views of sin have robbed men and women of seeing how desperately they need Jesus Christ as Savior to save them from sin.

In our culture we talk too glibly of the very thing against which God throws His most powerful denunciations and utters His strongest warnings. Sin is not to be regarded merely as a human weakness. When we speak of sin as an accident, God calls it an abomination. When we speak of sin as a blunder, God boldly declares it to be blindness. We call sin a trifle, but God insists that it is a tragedy.

Too often we seek to excuse ourselves in our sins, but God seeks to convict us of sin and save us from it. Sin then is not a toy with which to play but a terror to be shunned.

How Do I Redeem Myself?

A troubled young girl asked a question to anyone who would listen: "How can I redeem myself for what I've done? I'm not religious, and I've done a lot of bad things that I can't apologize for."

Someone answered back, "You should do good things in your life, help other people when you can. Be understanding and compassionate. Work hard, do almost any job that will benefit society, and you'll set things right for yourself."

Another person answered flippantly, "You don't have a soul, so don't worry about it."

A third person thought her answer would give the girl comfort and said, "Seek forgiveness of those you hurt and forgive yourself."

Though we may forgive ourselves, it will never win eternal life in Heaven with Jesus Christ. God has provided the way for every soul who desires to be rescued, turning from sin to be redeemed. Jesus said, "[I have] come to seek and to save that which was lost" (Luke 19:10). What are we rescued from? The sin that so easily plagues us. Sin leads to death and ultimately eternal separation from God in the place called Hell. Oh, I know that many people reject the idea of Hell, but Hell is not an idea— it is a reality.

This young lady cannot redeem what doesn't belong to her, for her soul belongs to God, who judges the soul. If she forgives her own wrongdoing toward others, her words will be empty and have no power. The nagging force of guilt still will follow her.

Asking others to forgive her is certainly a good start, but they have no power over their own souls, much less someone else's. Only the Lord Jesus can redeem the soul that is steeped in guilt and shame. This baggage weighs us down until we accept Jesus' gift—the gift that liberates souls from sin's power.

We cannot forgive sin because sin is against God. Only He can forgive and set us free. Good deeds will not bring comfort to the soul because the bad and hurtful things we do to others are ultimately done against the One who created our souls.

Your soul belongs to God. He is the only One who can redeem your soul.

It is God who made your soul.

It is the Lord Jesus who died to redeem your soul.

And it is the Holy Spirit who can fill your soul with God's love and guide you through life.

This is the way to have victory over sin.

An Appetite for Sin

From the beginning of time, people have wrestled with the power of sin. It comes in many forms: pride, jealousy, immorality, and every other form of self-satisfaction. These all stem from the root of original sin, and just as Satan appealed to Eve's appetite for the only thing God withheld, so Satan stands before us with lies. He tells us that doing the right thing according to God's standard only keeps us from happiness and self-satisfaction.

Describing the progression of sin, the Bible says: "But each one is tempted when he is drawn away by his own desires and enticed. Then, when desire has conceived, it gives birth to sin; and sin, when it is full-grown, brings forth death" (James 1:14–15). While Satan tempts our desires, he stirs up our appetites for sin. When we give in to the desire, he scores a victory, and we experience miserable defeat.

But it doesn't need to happen that way. Jesus Christ overcame the power of Satan on the cross. He died for you and for me. He was victorious over death because He defeated sin.

God will not tolerate sin. He condemns it and demands payment for it. God could not remain a righteous God and ignore sin. His holiness and His justice demand retribution. The tendency today is to feel that such a statement is too severe. So we find ourselves manufacturing another gospel. We may say that sin is not so bad. But God said *all* sin is very bad and demands the death penalty.

You may say, "That's pretty harsh." It is indeed—so harsh that God's love determined to send Someone who would pay the most brutal penalty. That Someone is the Lord Jesus Christ. He came willingly. Jesus, the perfect Son of God—who knew no sin—chose to bear our sins Himself. The Bible says, "He made Him who knew no sin to be sin for us, that we might become the righteousness of God in Him" (2 Corinthians 5:21).

The very fact that God sent His only Son to the cross in order to pay for sin shows that sin must be dark and black indeed in the sight of God. "But God demonstrates His own love toward us, in that while we were still sinners, Christ died for us" (Romans 5:8). "The Lord Jesus Christ, who gave himself for our sins," is the One who will "rescue us from the present evil age" (Galatians 1:3–4 NIV).

This is the wonderful story of the cross. Jesus paid the debt of our sins on the cross of Calvary to free us from having to suffer the penalty due us. People have turned their souls over to Satan, but from the cross of Christ we can hear the Savior say, "I have come to rescue you . . . come to Me. I bear the weight and the marks of your sin to set you free." He went willingly to the cross to recover the ownership of your soul. Christ paid the highest price with His precious blood to ransom all who are lost in sin.

Who Can Set Us Free?

Then what is the problem, you may ask? If Jesus died on the cross for our sin and God has forgiven us, then all is well, right?

If we were to take this position we would be as Adam and Eve, unwilling to admit our disobedience against God.

We must acknowledge before Him our transgressions. We must accept responsibility for our sin. Our hearts must truly be repentant for our rebellion against a holy God. We must realize repenting of our sin is our only hope of receiving God's salvation. And then we must turn from a life of sin to a life of truth and walk according to His truth. The Bible tells us clearly that all of us as sinners must repent and turn from our sin. "Let everyone who names the name of Christ depart from iniquity" (2 Timothy 2:19).

Repentance is more than just being sorry for our sin; it is a complete turning away from our total depravity. When we do that, Jesus Christ frees us from the consequences of sin, which is guilt and ultimate eternal separation from His presence. Only then are we delivered from the clutches of Satan and from His eternal dominion of Hell.

Perhaps you are saying, "Billy, this is archaic, hard to believe. You're asking me to believe that Someone I've never seen can forgive me of what I've done out in the open or even in private?" Jesus said, "Blessed are those who have not seen and yet have believed" (John 20:29).

Few people have ever met the ruler of a kingdom or a head of state. But the power of those leaders is real and affects all who live under their governance. Jesus Christ governs with love that demands obedience. His great love calls us to the foot of His cross so that we may receive His pardon for our transgressions. The Bible says, "Let the peace of God rule in your hearts" (Colossians 3:15).

WHO DOESN'T SEEK A PARDON?

You may be surprised to know that many nations around the world make provision for pardoning criminals. The constitution of Spain, for instance, forbids general pardons but states that "individual pardons are a gracious measure granted to sentenced convicts by the King."[8] South Africa's constitution gives the president the right to pardon a person for wrongdoing.[9] However, "the pardon process is . . . not available to persons who maintain their innocence and is not an advanced form of appeal procedure."[10]

Would you be surprised to learn that not everyone who is offered a pardon accepts it? Who, you might ask, would refuse a pardon? The answer is those who would, perhaps, refuse to be saved from a sinking ship. There are people who actually believe they can do no wrong; people who believe they can save themselves from anyone or anything.

From the records of the US Supreme Court comes such a story of defiance. In 1829, a man by the name of George Wilson was indicted for robbing the mail in Pennsylvania and endangering the life of a government mail carrier. For this crime "against the peace and dignity of the United States of America," Wilson was tried and sentenced to death.[11] But the president of the United States sent Wilson a pardon, stating:

I, Andrew Jackson, President of the United States of America . . . have pardoned . . . George Wilson the crime for which he has been sentenced to suffer death, remitting the penalty [as stated]. . . .

In testimony whereof I have hereunto set my hand and caused the seal of the United States to be affixed to these presents.[12]

At that point Wilson did a strange thing: he refused to accept the pardon. No one seemed to know what to do, so Wilson's case was sent to the Supreme Court.

After reviewing the facts of the case, Chief Justice John Marshall delivered the court's opinion that the value of a pardon is determined by the acceptance of the one receiving it and that, if refused, the pardon does not stand. The chief justice concluded that Wilson must be hanged. And he was.[13] Chief Justice Marshall wrote that

a pardon is an act of grace, proceeding from the power entrusted with the execution of the laws, which exempts the individual on whom it is bestowed from the punishment the law inflicts for a crime he has committed. It is the private, though official, act of the executive magistrate, delivered to the individual for whose benefit it is intended.[14]

Marshall further indicated that a pardon could not be forced upon Wilson, stating, "It may be supposed that no [one] being condemned to death would reject a pardon."[15] But George Wilson did, and Marshall's decision granted him the right to do that. But Marshall also made note of British law with regard to pardons, stating that a man usually must make a plea for pardon from the king. But even if an English felon waived the right to pardon, the king could still choose not to punish the felon because "the King has an interest in the life of his subject."[16]

This is a picture of God in Heaven, the supreme Judge who has a divine interest in His creation and offers abundant grace. Our crimes against Him—our sins—are forgivable. We must come to the foot of the cross and place our faith and trust in Jesus Christ, repenting of our sins.

When we look up to the Savior, He looks into our hearts and says, "I have already forgiven you. The blood I have shed will wash away your guilt." The Bible says, "The Son of Man [Jesus] has power on earth to forgive sins" (Matthew 9:6).

This is the story of the cross. As Peter put it, Jesus "'himself bore our sins' in his body on the tree, so that we might die to sins and live for righteousness; 'by his wounds you have been healed'" (1 Peter 2:24 NIV).

GOD V. YOU

Jesus stands ready to forgive you, pardon your offense against Him, and receive you into His care. His will is to save men and women, not condemn them; for He has a profound interest in His creation, so much so that He paid your penalty and mine.

Every sinner must come to an hour of decision.

We are criminals by conviction. We are imprisoned by law. The King is willing to grant us mercy for our offenses. He has made provision to forgive our sinful deeds, and He offers us His grace. Failing to respond to God's grace will have devastating consequences.

So in the case of *God v. you*, do you make the plea for Jesus Christ to save you? He will if you admit your guilt and accept His pardon, then live for Him now and with Him in eternity. Or will you reject the pardon? Will you try to convince yourself and others of your innocence?

Satan is the one who has convinced you that you are blameless, and you go on dying, a little more each day in your guilt and despair, without hope. God desires to give you eternal life, free from the guilt of sin, but Satan desires your very soul to be forever lost with him.

You can be freed from Satan's stronghold. You can be acquitted of the penalty of death. This is why the Bible says, "For he has rescued us from the dominion of darkness and brought us into the kingdom of the Son he loves, in whom we have redemption, the forgiveness of sins" (Colossians 1:13–14 NIV).

You don't have to spend the rest of your life on earth and through eternity imprisoned by your guilt. You can be pardoned. And when the King pardons, your name appears in Heaven's record, the Book of Life. "For Christ also suffered once for sins, the just for the unjust, that He might bring us to God" (1 Peter 3:18). This is an eternal exchange: sin and death for hope and eternal life.

Do You Have Enough Faith to Accept a Pardon?

Many say, "This is too hard to comprehend." May I say to you that it cannot be understood without believing by faith? Faith is the key that unlocks this great and wonderful truth of God's bountiful grace.

The world is blinded to the fact that God's redemption of humanity through His Son is limited. It is only as we accept Christ as our personal Savior by faith that we are born again—given new life in Christ—and are thus brought into the family of God. Scripture teaches that "all are justified freely by his grace through the redemption that came by Christ Jesus. God presented Christ as a sacrifice of atonement, through the shedding of his blood—to be received by faith" (Romans 3:24–25 NIV).

"All" is a wonderful truth—don't miss it. The Bible's message is inclusive—for *all*. God's message is also exclusive—only those who call upon His name can be saved. But God's Word makes it clear that He desires that *all* be saved.

E. Stanley Jones, the Methodist evangelist and missionary who was twice nominated for the Nobel Peace Prize for his reconciling work around the world, wrote, "At the cross God wrapped his heart in flesh and blood and let it be nailed to the cross for our redemption."[17]

The notion of sin and the nature of sin have been debated from the beginning of time, and that debate continues in our present culture. Sin presents itself in the mind, manifests itself in word and deed, and is hidden in the heart of all of us. It will overtake the man and woman who refuse to believe it will conquer them.

The Bible says that the whole world is a prisoner of sin.

> Before the coming of this faith, we were held in custody under the law, locked up until the faith that was to come would be revealed. So the law was our guardian until Christ came that we might be justified by faith. Now that this faith has come, we are no longer under a guardian. (Galatians 3:23–25 NIV)

Sin has crippled human nature, but God has provided the cure. There is no sin that the blood of Jesus Christ cannot cleanse. And that's good news indeed for a culture that still doesn't know what to do with sin. WHY WOULD ANYONE REFUSE SUCH A PARDON?

For the grace of God that brings salvation has appeared to all men . . . denying ungodliness . . . looking for the blessed hope.
(TITUS 2:11–13)

CHAPTER FOUR

THE PRICE OF VICTORY

[Jesus] became the author of eternal salvation
to all who obey Him, called by God.

—HEBREWS 5:9–10

WHO DOESN'T LIKE BEING ON A VICTORY TEAM? Victory is something we all want to experience. In fact, I have never met anyone who would choose defeat over victory. Human nature strives for victory. The late Paul "Bear" Bryant, award-winning coach at the University of Alabama said, "The price of victory is high but so are the rewards."[1] Another Paul, the great apostle, said, "I press toward the goal for the prize of the upward call of God in Christ Jesus" (Philippians 3:14).

What is the greatest and most costly battle ever to take place? Who was the victor, and what was the reward? The greatest battle ever fought was between good and evil. This great battle took place at Golgotha—also known as Mount Calvary—a rugged hill outside the walled city of Jerusalem. Jesus Christ was Victor, paying the cost with His blood. The reward was the salvation of human souls.

Jesus had spent three years with twelve chosen men—His disciples. He had walked with them across the plains and through the valleys. He had sailed with them upon the waters. He had sat with them on the mountains and taught them many things, including this: "The Son of Man will be betrayed to the chief priests and to the scribes; and they will condemn Him to death, and deliver Him to the Gentiles to mock and to scourge and to crucify. And the third day He will rise again" (Matthew 20:18–19).

Jesus gave them a glimpse of what was to happen, but they did not comprehend that the Man they believed to be their King could ever fall into the brutal hands of mere men. They were focused on the Friend they called Master—the One who preached salvation and a coming kingdom, the One whom they believed to be the promised Messiah.

VICTORY FROM BONDAGE

Passover in the city of Jerusalem was a day of remembrance—the holiest of days for the Jews. This day marked victory from generations of bondage, freedom from enslavement by the Egyptian kingdom. What the Jewish nation failed to realize, however, was it had exchanged physical enslavement in Egypt for religious ritual as well as Roman rule. Celebration of Passover for them was a time to remember God's intervention on their behalf to free them from their oppressors.

Jesus had been sent from Heaven to earth to identify with their suffering and to preach that His kingdom was not a human kingdom but the kingdom of God. He preached not religion but a personal relationship that God desired to have with people. They failed to see that God's law revealed humanity's sin. They didn't like to think of themselves as sinners. Pride in their religious heritage had blinded their eyes to the truth that they, too, were sinners in need of forgiveness. They continued the practice of the law and sacrifices offered for sins, unwilling to believe that Jesus had come to fulfill the law (Matthew 5:17) by cleansing it with His blood.

Many who followed Jesus loved the miracles that He performed. They loved His message of peace and love. But while they continued their sacrifices, they rejected the idea that their Messiah would have to offer Himself as the ultimate sacrifice for sin. They had missed the purpose of the sacrificial system, of slaying an innocent and unblemished lamb whose blood would cover sin, that for centuries had pointed toward the cross. From the beginning this foreshadowed "the Lamb of God who takes away the sin of the world" (John 1:29). The Bible says, "These are a shadow of the things that were to come; the reality, however, is found in Christ" (Colossians 2:17 NIV). But when Jesus spoke of His death and the cross, many turned away from Him, rejecting the truth that all men and women are sinners and must repent of their sins and follow Him by faith.

Resounding Victory

As Passover approached that year, "all the chief priests and elders of the people plotted against Jesus to put Him to death" (Matthew 27:1). This brewing storm overshadowed the celebration that was taking place in the city. Jerusalem was the destination for travelers who had come to observe the most religious holiday in the land. It was to be a time of remembrance, proclaiming that they were the people of God. Instead they became a mob who cried out for the blood of God's Son—the very One who had come to redeem them from the bondage of sin and the law they could not keep.

No one there that day would ever have thought such chaos would result in resounding victory. How could such a cataclysmic event as the crucifixion of Jesus Christ, robed in horror and brutality, turn out victorious? One must look into the greatest book ever written, the Bible, to find the truth.

People had turned the Feast of the Passover into a furious exhibition. Can you imagine a carnival-like atmosphere, seeing a crowd gathered to watch someone be tortured to death? To most in the modern world, this would be unthinkable. But this is the picture we see in the Bible—a hostile crowd chanting for death. The people entertained themselves by demanding an innocent Man's murder while calling for a convicted prisoner's freedom.

This was no surprise to Jesus. He had told His disciples that He must die. He also told them that He would be victorious over death and the cross. But His words had been hard for them to comprehend.

The religious rulers had sought to find fault with Jesus. They demanded His death from the rulers of Rome. To keep peace in the city, Rome caved to the pressure of the Jews and sentenced Jesus to a Roman-style execution—on a cross.

THE OLD RUGGED CROSS

Some hang gold crosses around their necks. Others admire such a symbol mounted on a majestic cathedral. Some kneel by a cross of flowers plunged into the dirt at a loved one's gravesite. But on Passover that day the masses swarmed a pathway that led from the city gate, following the innocent Man bearing an old rugged cross, a symbol of agony, an instrument of shame. And it was a scandalous cross that Jesus bore for you and for me.

The Bible tells us that after being ruthlessly beaten, Jesus was handed over to soldiers who laid a cross upon His flesh-torn back. Jesus wore the heaviness of man's sin upon His shoulders. He bore in His heart the ache for lost souls. He agonized under the tremendous weight as He ascended Golgotha's hill.

The people had not believed Jesus when He had said, "I am the way" (John 14:6). Yet they followed and pressed in on Him, mocking and ridiculing. The crowd had dismissed the truth when He had proclaimed, "I am . . . the truth" (John 14:6). And as Truth climbed the craggy mountain, the people cried, "Crucify Him, crucify Him!" (Luke 23:21). They had been victorious in their demands that Pilate end the life of the Man who came to give life. They had not believed Jesus when He had said, "I am . . . the life" (John 14:6). And their taunting grew louder: "Crucify Him, crucify Him!"

Jesus stumbled beneath the tree upon which He would die for the sins of even those who falsely accused Him and mercilessly condemned Him to death. This instrument of death—the cross—would become a stumbling block to the rebellious and the mercy seat for the redeemed. Forgiveness and mercy for sinners—you and me—is what Jesus delivered from the cross. That is the victory of the cross.

Imagine the scene. Throngs of people were milling about, shouting over the gruesome sound of a mallet pounding spikes through the hands that had brought healing and feet that had walked on water. Some of the people gawking that day had perhaps witnessed His miracles; nearly all had heard of the great things He had done.

The cross of Jesus was hoisted up and plunged into the ground— the place of His crucifixion. The jolt would have caused unimaginable anguish. Jesus was raised up as a spectacle before violent spectators. There He hung in shame and reproach. On this most holy day, when no work was to be done or business transacted, man's most unholy work was done.

But Jesus had told His followers to expect this. "'And I, if I am lifted up from the earth, will draw all peoples to Myself.' This He said, signifying by what death He would die" (John 12:32–33). The weight of His body ripped away His flesh from the stakes thrust through Him. His very blood was poured out, staining the wood. His heart labored to beat as He looked down upon human hearts filled with sin.

Nailed to the Cross

What did Jesus see from the cross? Mockers. His penetrating eyes looked into eyes blinded to the truth. He saw the religious leaders gaping at Him as they read the title nailed above His head, with the charge against Him written in three languages: "THIS IS JESUS THE KING OF THE JEWS" (Matthew 27:37).

Intended to mock Jesus, the sign actually proclaimed the greatest truth: Jesus died for all. The title was written in Hebrew so the religious would understand. It was written in Greek so the cultured could understand. It was written in Latin so world government could understand.

The message of the cross is for everyone. "For God did not send His Son into the world to condemn the world, but that the world through Him might be saved" (John 3:17). The cross shows the seriousness of our sin, but it also proclaims the immeasurable love of God. Jesus says to the human race, "I will meet you at only one place, and that's the cross—the place of victory."

THE FOOT OF THE CROSS

Jesus looked at the crowd gathered, but most of His followers had fled. His disciples, except John, had deserted Him. The only solemn presence was found in the agonized faces and shattered hearts of Jesus' mother, some other women, and a few friends who stood watching in horror.

Jesus watched as the Roman guards gambled for His garments at the foot of the cross. No doubt during their rowdy game, they glanced up toward the heavens, watching Jesus, whom they had flogged, bleeding and gasping for breath in the heat of day. The Bible says, "Sitting down, they kept watch over Him there" (Matthew 27:36).

On either side of Jesus hung two criminals—thieves and murderers—who in spite of their own pain found strength to slander Him. One said, "If You are the Christ, save Yourself and us" (Luke 23:39). Others who passed by hurled insults at Him, saying, "Save Yourself! If You are the Son of God, come down from the cross" (Matthew 27:40).

The chief priests, teachers of the law, and the elders sneered, "He saved others; Himself He cannot save. Let the Christ, the King of Israel, descend now from the cross, that we may see and believe" (Mark 15:31–32). The soldiers also mocked him and said, "If You are the King of the Jews, save Yourself" (Luke 23:37). They puffed themselves up as they carried out the gore and shame of crucifying an innocent Man.

This wasn't a somber scene, where people comforted the dying. This was a scandalous scheme, where bloodthirsty people gathered to falsely accuse the very One who represented eternal life. Hatred and hostility permeated the atmosphere. The crowd delighted in jeering Him who had come to save them from evil. This is what Jesus saw and heard from the cross. He saw the wickedness of the people's hearts. He heard the vile reproach from their lips.

You may rightly say, "This is not a picture of victory."

It is only when we hear the words that came from His lips that we can rejoice in what it all meant that day, what it still means today.

What did the Master say to the soldiers who tortured Him?

What did the Son of God say to His Father who had forsaken Him?

What did Jesus say to His mother who grieved?

What did the King of the Jews say to the religious leaders who called out to Him?

What did the Son of Man say to those who taunted Him?

From the same lips that spoke peace during His three-year ministry, Jesus spoke love to His friends as well as His enemies.

THE MESSAGE FROM THE CROSS

Jesus willingly died on the cross to identify with all those searching for truth. Are you among them? Have you heard what Jesus has said to you from the cross? You were there. I was there. Oh, it's true that we hadn't been born yet, but our sins were present that day. It wasn't just the soldiers, thieves, religious leaders, and passersby who took part in the crucifixion of Jesus Christ. Our sins also nailed Him to the tree.

No one could have forced Jesus to the cross had He been unwilling to go. This is the crux of the cross—Jesus chose to go to Calvary. He willingly laid down His life for the sins of the world. He died of His own volition by allowing your sins and my sins to be nailed to His cross.

The Bible says that we are doomed to eternal banishment from the presence of God because sin separates man from God. Remember, sin brings about a penalty: "The soul who sins shall die" (Ezekiel 18:20). But Jesus Christ said, "I will die in their place. I'll take their judgment. I'll take their death. I'll go to the cross." This is what Christ did for you and for me. Two thousand years ago, God invited a morally corrupt world to the foot of the cross. There He held your sins and mine to the flames until every last vestige of our guilt was consumed.

When Jesus hung on the cross, a great unseen cosmic battle raged in the heavens. And in the end Christ triumphed over all the forces of evil and death and Hell, giving us the greatest of all hope—eternal forgiveness.

Though the cross repels, it also attracts. It possesses a magnetic quality. Once you have been to the cross, you will never be the same. The greatest vision of sin is at the cross, where we also see the greatest vision of love. "Greater love has no one than this, than to lay down one's life for his friends" (John 15:13). Jesus hung from the cross with us in mind. And as He hung there, He preached the most powerful sermon. In just seven brief phrases, He encapsulated the totality of His three-year ministry.

JESUS, THE GREAT FORGIVER

The first message Jesus preached from the cross was forgiveness.

Crucifixion is an evil death. The position of the victim on the cross results in asphyxia, prohibiting adequate exhalation and inhalation of air. Breathing is laborious and speaking insufferable. Yet in the midst of this agony, Jesus ministered to humanity's vilest and also to the brokenhearted. This is why the cross is often seen as the symbol of Christianity.

As the guards divided His garments by casting lots, Jesus said,

"Father, forgive them, for they do not know what they do" (Luke 23:34). Even from the cross, Jesus spoke to His Heavenly Father on behalf of His enemies. This was a message Jesus' followers had struggled with: "But I say to you, love your enemies, bless those who curse you, do good to those who hate you, and pray for those who spitefully use you and persecute you, that you may be sons of your Father in heaven" (Matthew 5:44–45).

The cross throws a great searchlight on the evil of the world. We don't want the searchlight of the cross examining our hearts, telling us that we're guilty before God. The blood of Jesus convicts, but it also cleanses. The blood of Jesus brings reproach, but it also brings redemption. The blood of Jesus frustrates evil, but it also brings forgiveness to the sinner. The blood of Jesus cancels God's judgment on the repentant heart.

JESUS, THE GREAT SAVIOR

The second message Jesus preached was of salvation and assurance. As Jesus emptied out His life's blood, He heard the thieves on either side of Him debating what they had heard about the Christ. One rejected salvation with sarcasm. But the other received Him:

> Then one of the criminals . . . blasphemed Him, saying, "If You are the Christ, save Yourself and us."
>
> But the other, answering, rebuked him, saying, "Do you not even fear God, seeing you are under the same condemnation? And we indeed justly, for we receive the due reward of our deeds; but this Man has done nothing wrong." Then he said to Jesus, "Lord, remember me when You come into Your kingdom."
>
> And Jesus said to him, "Assuredly, I say to you, today you will be with Me in Paradise." (Luke 23:39–43)

Jesus knew the hearts of these convicted criminals, but only one became convicted of his sin. The Bible says conviction leads to repentance.

The thief, who no doubt also labored to speak, confessed his sins, admitting that his deeds deserved the punishment of death. He acknowledged that Jesus was innocent of all wrongdoing. And by asking to be received in Jesus' kingdom, he proclaimed that Jesus truly was the King.

The Bible says,

> "The word is near you, in your mouth and in your heart" (that is, the word of faith which we preach): that if you confess with your mouth the Lord Jesus and believe in your heart that God has raised Him from the dead, you will be saved. For with the heart one believes unto righteousness, and with the mouth confession is made unto salvation. For the Scripture says, "Whoever believes on Him will not be put to shame." For there is no distinction between Jew and Greek, for the same Lord over all is rich to all who call upon Him. (Romans 10:8–12)

The thief displayed this remarkable faith. He was hanging near the cross of Christ, and the very Word—the Lord Jesus—was near him, receiving his repentant heart.

The only deathbed repentance in the whole Bible is this account of the thief on the cross. I have known a few people who accepted Christ as their Savior just before drawing their last breath. But my friend, do not presume on the grace of God, for the Scripture says, "Now is the accepted time; behold, now is the day of salvation" (2 Corinthians 6:2).

Nowhere in Scripture are we promised tomorrow. The Scripture doesn't say that tomorrow is the day of salvation, for that would tempt us to continue in sin for another day. Do you understand the urgency and necessity of salvation? The thief understood that more than being bound to the cross of death, he was at the crossroads of decision. He chose the only path to salvation, for salvation comes only through the cross of Christ. Christ is the way, His word is the truth, and His death and resurrection bring life.

There weren't many that day thinking of the promised resurrection.

But the words of the thief revealed his faith in that glorious hope. In the midst of suffering, surrounded by vile men, Jesus was pleased to hear the sincere words of repentance, "Lord, remember me when You come into Your kingdom."

This sinner hanging near the cross of Jesus found salvation that very hour. In his letter to the Romans, Paul quoted from the Old Testament:

> Whoever calls on the name of the LORD
> Shall be saved.
>
> (JOEL 2:32)

The thief would never have the opportunity to walk in the ways of Christ on earth, but for more than two thousand years his testimony of what Jesus Christ did for him has spoken from the pages of Scripture—just as the psalm foretold:

> Future generations will be told about the Lord.
> They will proclaim his righteousness,
> declaring to a people yet unborn:
> He has done it!
>
> (PSALM 22:30–31 NIV)

The Savior willingly poured out His blood for the sin of humanity, knowing that "without the shedding of blood there is no forgiveness of sins" (Hebrews 9:22 ESV). This criminal turned convert exhibited faith beyond reason. Faith means that you totally commit to Christ. Your hope is in Him alone. He becomes the One in whom you trust completely for your salvation. The Scripture says, "So then faith comes by hearing, and hearing by the word of God" (Romans 10:17).

We see the contrast between these two criminals and their responses to Jesus. Both saw Him unjustly condemned. Both heard His message from the cross. Jesus saw into the hearts of these two men just as He sees into our hearts today. His arms were stretched out as if to say, "Come."

His ears were not dull. He heard the insults of rejection, and He heard the faint plea of repentance:

> Behold, the LORD's hand is not shortened,
> That it cannot save;
> Nor His ear heavy,
> That it cannot hear.
>
> (ISAIAH 59:1)

There are two classes of people in the world: the saved and the lost. Both have the same opportunity to choose Christ or reject Him. These two criminals represent all human beings, all having the same choice. The one who rejected Christ cursed Him while the other confessed Him. The latter knew he deserved death, but in his own weakness he exhibited the faith to believe that Jesus Christ was indeed the Savior of the world. The Bible says, "For indeed the gospel was preached to us as well as to them; but the word which they heard did not profit them, not being mixed with faith in those who heard it" (Hebrews 4:2).

Repentance is by faith, believing that God will forgive. Repentance is acknowledging your sin and by faith, accepting Christ's forgiveness, changing your mind about who Jesus Christ is and what He has done for you, then turning from sin and going the way of the cross. When you do this, He empowers you to believe that He will cleanse you from sin and give you a new heart, a renewed mind, and the will to follow Him into His kingdom.

This convert had a change of attitude. As Jesus was finishing His work on the cross, this man was a few breaths from death, and he was promised a new beginning—eternal life in paradise—in the presence of God.

When we read the account of the crucifixion, it is easy to miss the glory of the cross because of its shame—shame for human sin that nailed Jesus to the tree. The cross represents the suffering love of God, which bears the guilt of humanity's sin, which alone is able to melt the sinner's heart and bring him to repentance for salvation. This is the glory of the cross.

It has been said that there was a cross in the heart of God long before the cross was erected at Calvary. There is overwhelming wonder at the greatness of God's love for us found at the foot of that cross.

JESUS, THE GREAT COMFORTER

The third message Jesus preached was that of comfort, despite the anguish He endured. The nails that pierced the hands and feet of Jesus were not nearly as painful as man's sin, which pierced the heart of Jesus. Yet the blood that flowed from Jesus' veins was as precious as the love that flowed from His heart to save the souls of many.

Jesus' flesh scorched in the blaze of the sun, yet He preached comfort as He had done so many times. Jesus set aside His own distress to care for and make provision for His mother. He knew that His disciples had deserted Him, yet when He looked down from the cross, He saw that one had returned to Mary's side: "When Jesus therefore saw His mother, and the disciple whom He loved standing by, He said to His mother, 'Woman, behold your son!' Then He said to the disciple, 'Behold your mother!' And from that hour that disciple [John] took her to his own home" (John 19:26–27).

The night before, Jesus had promised His disciples that He would not leave His own "comfortless" (John 14:18 KJV). Even from the cross of His suffering, we see Jesus nurturing relationships and giving hope. For this is precisely why He died: to bring mankind back into fellowship with His Father in Heaven.

We are told that "the Son of Man did not come to be served, but to serve, and to give His life a ransom for many" (Matthew 20:28). Jesus Himself had said this to His disciples, and on the cross we see Jesus exemplifying His word of truth.

While Jesus was crucified by sinful people, His death was voluntary: "No one takes [My life] from Me, but I lay it down of Myself. I have power to lay it down, and I have power to take it again" (John 10:18).

Jesus did so to fulfill the prophecy found in the book of Isaiah, written five hundred years earlier, that the Lamb of God would be led away to the slaughter:

> He was despised and rejected by mankind,
>   a man of suffering, and familiar with pain. . . .
>   he was despised, and we held him in low esteem.
>
> Surely he took up our pain
>   and bore our suffering,
> yet we considered him punished by God,
>   stricken by him, and afflicted.
> But he was pierced for our transgressions,
>   he was crushed for our iniquities;
> the punishment that brought us peace was on him,
>   and by his wounds we are healed. . . .
>
> He poured out his life unto death,
>   and was numbered with the transgressors.
> For he bore the sin of many,
>   and made intercession for the transgressors.
>
> (ISAIAH 53:3–5, 12 NIV)

Jesus today is seated at the right hand of His Father in Heaven, making intercession for those who belong to Him. His words are still bringing comfort to those who, like Mary, are overcome with despair, overwrought with pain, and overlooked by others. Jesus came to identify with us in all of these things and give hope. The Bible says,

> Because of the LORD's great love we are not consumed,
>   for his compassions never fail.
> They are new every morning;
>   great is *your* faithfulness. . . .

> The LORD is good to those whose hope is in him,
>   to the one who seeks him;
> it is good to wait quietly
>   for the salvation of the LORD.
>   (LAMENTATIONS 3:22–26 NIV, AUTHOR'S EMPHASIS)

It is impossible to imagine the ripping pain Mary must have felt as she watched her Son bleeding, suffering an agonizing death; heard His last words; and was helpless to comfort Him. Surely, if anyone could have the full assurance that Jesus' death would end in victory, it was Mary, for she knew beyond any doubt that Jesus had been conceived of the Holy Spirit. She knew beyond the shadow of the cross that Jesus the Son of God would live again.

JESUS, THE GREAT RECONCILER

The fourth message from the cross was one of reconciliation. Jesus, who knew no sin, had to deal with sin in order to reconcile man to God. In this darkest hour, reconciliation was victoriously won.

What must have gone through Mary's mind when she heard the wailing voices directed at Jesus? His accusers shouted, "Let God rescue him now if he wants him, for he said, 'I am the Son of God'" (Matthew 27:43 NIV). But Jesus did not come down from the cross. God the Father did not rescue Him. Why? Because Jesus willingly gave up His life to save others.

When Jesus' disciples refused the previous night to believe that He would be crucified on a cross, Jesus had said to them, "Now my soul is troubled, and what shall I say? 'Father, save me from this hour'? No, it was for this very reason I came to this hour. Father, glorify your name!" (John 12:27–28 NIV). He could have called legions of angels to His side. But He chose to die in order to spare us eternal death. He chose to suffer to grant us comfort. He chose to give up His earthly life that we might have everlasting life. This is my hope. Is it yours?

Jesus suffered the persecution of His own people. He suffered desertion by His own disciples. But worse than all that, He suffered abandonment from His Father in Heaven for the glory of God. No wonder Jesus cried out from the cross, "My God, My God, why have You forsaken Me?" (Mark 15:34). God the Son never had been separated from God the Father, and Jesus felt the horrific pain of isolation as He endured God's wrath upon the evil of sin.

Eyes were blinded. Hearts were like stone. Ears were deaf to the truth. On the cross Jesus was severely afflicted with the sins of the world, but it was also on the cross that He completed the greatest of all of His works. The cross is where sin met the Savior. The cross is where the sinner finds salvation. The cross is where wretched souls can find victory in Jesus.

Jesus endured grief that cannot be fathomed. This is the bloodstained picture of sin that separates men and women from fellowship with God. We must crucify—put to death—our ways and go the way of the cross. When we do that, we participate in His great work of reconciliation.

Jesus, the Great Thirst Quencher

As Jesus' time was at hand, He preached the fifth message from the cross: "I thirst!" (John 19:28). Just imagine His parched lips, His blistering skin, every ligament, tendon, and muscle burning from being stretched out on a cruel cross. He had been whipped beyond recognition even before being nailed to the tree. In severe distress, He writhed from inflamed wounds, immense grief, and fatigue of body, soul, and spirit, culminating in nature's deepest need to quench insufferable thirst.

But the soldiers' hearts were hardened; they continued to antagonize. One of them dipped a sponge in wine vinegar and lifted it up to Jesus on a stalk of the hyssop plant. But I believe there was something Jesus thirsted for more; everything He did and said pointed to His passion to save lost souls. Jesus thirsted for souls.

This had been evident earlier in His ministry when He journeyed into Samaria. The Bible says in John 4 that it was late in the day—"about the sixth hour" (v. 6)—and Jesus was weary and thirsty. He sat down near Jacob's well, and a woman came to draw water. Jesus asked her for a drink . . . but His aim was to speak to her about her soul. The woman was troubled by Jesus' request because she knew that Jews did not associate with Samaritans. "How is it that You, being a Jew, ask a drink from me, a Samaritan woman?" (v. 9). They conversed a bit more, and then Jesus told her something that changed her life: "Whoever drinks of this [well] water will thirst again, but whoever drinks of the water that I shall give him will never thirst. But the water that I shall give him will become in him a fountain of water springing up into everlasting life" (vv. 13–14).

Now we look at Jesus on the cross, at about the sixth hour, saying, "I thirst." The enemy lifted up sour vinegar, representing the sourness of sin. Jesus had taken the cup of sin's wrath, completing His earthly mission. In that moment He grappled with Hell, judgment, sin, and death; and He defeated them all. He had come to rescue and to save the lost. His accusers had intended the cross for harm, "but God intended it for good to accomplish what is now being done, the saving of many lives" (Genesis 50:20 NIV). And to do that, He had to die that we might live.

That is why I love to gaze at the cross. In it we see the expression of the greatest love of God for man. The Lord "turned the curse into a blessing for you, because the LORD your God loves you" (Deuteronomy 23:5). Jesus, the Living Water, sustains and nourishes our weary souls.

JESUS, THE FURNISHER AND FINISHER OF OUR FAITH

The sixth message from the lips of Jesus was that His work on the cross was complete. He had satisfied the penalty for sin through His own death and had completed His rescue mission to redeem the souls of men. Now He could sound the victory cry: "It is finished!" (John 19:30).

What was finished? Certainly not Jesus' life, for He had told the disciples that He would die and be raised on the third day. It was the payment of sin that was finished—paid in full by the willing sacrifice of Jesus's own blood to redeem man's soul. "You were not redeemed with corruptible things . . . but with the precious blood of Christ, as of a lamb without blemish and without spot" (1 Peter 1:18–19).

Jesus was not forced to lay down His life to pay for sin. He gave Himself as the substitutionary lamb, the Lamb of God slain for the world, just as the Bible says, and He is now the Shepherd of souls. "For you were like sheep going astray, but have now returned to the Shepherd and Overseer of your souls" (1 Peter 2:25).

The Bible also says, "When he had received the drink, Jesus said, 'It is finished.' With that, he bowed his head and gave up his spirit" (John 19:30 NIV). On His own accord, He quietly, reverently, and deliberately bowed His head, knowing He had finished the work His Father had given Him to do.

"It is finished" is a proclamation of salvation's completed plan. Never again will blood be shed for sin. Jesus Christ has paid the ransom.

Had Jesus been rescued from the cross by His Father, the ransom for sin would have never been paid. For this profound reason, God had sent Jesus on a rescue mission to save the souls of mankind, and Jesus was obedient to the Father's calling. God the Father and God the Son are one, unified in bringing about the great gift of our salvation, our victory, found in the God-Man Jesus Christ.

How mysteriously wonderful it is that Christ willingly took your place and mine. We now have the opportunity to finish with the hope and certainty of eternal life because of victory in the cross of Christ—"looking unto Jesus, the author and finisher of our faith" (Hebrews 12:2).

JESUS, THE GREAT VICTOR

In Scripture the number seven is symbolic of completion. Jesus began His seven-point sermon from the cross by calling on His Father, and

He concluded this life-changing message in the Father's name. Most of those around Him paid no attention—until the sixth hour. Night had not fallen, but the sun stopped shining, and darkness covered the land. Jesus cried out with the voice of victory, "'Father, "into Your hands I commit My spirit."' Having said this, He breathed His last" (Luke 23:46).

Jesus, who had been delivered into the hands of sinners, was now in the hands of God the Father. Sin had been crucified once and for all.

At that moment, the Bible says,

> the curtain of the temple was torn in two from top to bottom. The earth shook, the rocks split and the tombs broke open. The bodies of many holy people who had died were raised to life. . . .
>
> When the centurion and those with him who were guarding Jesus saw the earthquake and all that had happened, they were terrified, and exclaimed, "Surely he was the Son of God!" (Matthew 27:51–54 NIV)

And "when all the people who had gathered to witness this sight saw what took place, they beat their breasts and went away" (Luke 23:48 NIV). For this moment in time the gamblers and the grumblers, the scoffers and the swindlers, were silenced. Their excruciating assault of Jesus was now their unrelenting nightmare.

YOU WERE THERE

With whom do you identify at the cross of Jesus Christ? Are you just passing by, scoffing at what Christ has done for you, or are you thirsting for the life that Jesus longs to give you? Do you identify with the thief who rejected Christ as Lord or the thief who repented to Jesus the Savior?

There are some who might identify with the religious rulers who believed they were holy and righteous, yet in vengeance they betrayed, mocked, and murdered the Righteous One.

Perhaps you see yourself sitting with the soldiers, gambling for a little piece of Jesus; or standing with Mary and John, waiting to be comforted by Jesus. Will you go down in defeat as the executioners did when they felt the power of the earthquake that knocked them to their knees, or will you say with the centurion, "Surely He was the Son of God!"?

Are you standing near the cross with a heart wrenched in pain as you consider the Savior who shed His blood for you? Are you agonizing over your sins that nailed Jesus to the tree? He agonized for you. Are you willing to be persecuted for the name of Jesus? He was persecuted for you. He suffered for you. Will you commit your spirit into the hands of the One who died for you? Jesus looked down from the cross on our sin and loved us in spite of it. Will you look to Him and be saved (Isaiah 45:22)?

The Bible says that Jesus . . .

forgave us all our sins, having canceled the charge of our legal indebtedness, which stood against us and condemned us; he has taken it away, nailing it to the cross. And having disarmed the powers and authorities, he made a public spectacle of them, triumphing over them by the cross. (Colossians 2:13–15 NIV)

Jesus defeated sin, and His victory over death brings life and hope to the souls of men. Scripture tells us that "'death has been swallowed up in victory.' . . . The sting of death is sin, and the power of sin is the law. But thanks be to God! He gives us the victory through our Lord Jesus Christ" (1 Corinthians 15:54–57 NIV).

The price of victory was the precious blood of Jesus, and the reward is in the souls won for His Father's kingdom. Will you remain defeated by sin, or will you say, "I am finished with sin's hold on me and ready to take hold of Christ"?

THE SUFFERING CROSS OF JESUS IS STAINED WITH THE SINS OF THE WORLD, BUT THE GLORIOUS CROSS OF CHRIST CLEANSES SINNERS' HEARTS STAINED BY SIN, AND TO ALL WHO ARE SAVED, IT IS A TREE OF LIFE.

The LORD has made known His salvation;
His righteousness He has revealed in the sight of the nations.
(PSALM 98:2)

CHAPTER FIVE

WHERE IS JESUS?

*Nor is there salvation in any other, for there is no other name
under heaven given among men by which we must be saved.*

—ACTS 4:12

WHAT IS THE ULTIMATE VICTORY OF THE CROSS?
That it could not hold the Savior of the world, who
triumphed over sin and death, winning salvation for
mankind. The resurrection story of Jesus Christ is what gives meaning
and power to the cross. What a failure Christianity would be if it could
not carry our hopes beyond the coldness and depths of the grave. You
see, the resurrection means the salvation of our souls.

What does the resurrection mean to you? Many have never thought
about it. Some believe that Jesus died leaving a legacy of "Do good to
your neighbor," never believing that He was raised from the dead. Others
think the resurrection was a hoax. There are those who question whether
Jesus even existed. True believers in Jesus Christ have no doubt that He
lived among us, died for our sins, and after three days was resurrected to
life, conquering the sting of death, offering the human race the greatest
gift—His sacrificial love.

Several months ago an entertainment network carried a story on the Billy Graham Library, highlighting it as a point of interest in the city of Charlotte, North Carolina. The show's cohost, Kristy Villa, arrived on the property along with her crew and was met by a colleague who explained what visitors might experience while there. She drew the journalist's attention to the many crosses displayed, including the forty-foot glass cross through which visitors enter the building.

Halfway through the presentation Villa said with a sense of awe, "I see all the crosses, but where is Jesus?" The colleague smiled and said, "He's in Heaven, and He is also present in the lives of those who believe in Him and follow Him as their personal Lord and Savior." The journalist threw her hands around her face and exclaimed, "Oh, that's right! Some worship a crucifix, but Christians worship a risen Christ." After a moment Villa said, "I have been in church my whole life, but I have never heard the emphasis put on an empty cross."

She may not have realized it, but she had just proclaimed the heart of the Gospel, as I have done for more than seventy years, and later told her viewers, "This destination [the Library] is a place you must come and see!"[1] When I heard this marvelous report, it made my heart leap, and I thought about the words of the psalmist: "Come and see what God has done . . . for mankind!" (Psalm 66:5 NIV).

The question we must all answer is, "What does Jesus' work on the cross and His resurrection mean to us, and what does it mean to be saved?"

Many people, including some who claim to be Christians, do not fully grasp the impact that the crucified and risen Christ makes upon the human heart. How do I know this? Because there is no change in them. Have you asked yourself, "What do I believe about the empty cross and the empty tomb?"

The foot of the empty cross is the ultimate destination in life. Your acceptance of Jesus' sacrifice, or your rejection of it, determines your future life. If you do not believe that Jesus died for you, then you will remain the same, being gripped by sin and dying by its penalty, with certainty of eternal judgment in Hell and banishment from God. But if you believe that Jesus rose from the grave, achieving victory over the cross of death, and you accept that He paid your penalty, you will never be the same.

THE EMPTY CROSS IS FULL OF HOPE

The cross represents doom for sin and hope for sinners. It condemns sin and cleanses souls. The cross is where Jesus was crucified in our place and where Christ brings resurrection life to mankind. The bloodstained cross is gruesome to some, but the empty cross is full of hope.

Satan, overly eager to thwart God's purposes, overstepped his bounds, and God turned what seemed to be life's greatest tragedy into history's greatest triumph. The death of Christ, perpetrated by evil men, was thought by them to be the end, but His grave became but a doorway to a larger victory.

The resurrection empowers faith in Jesus Christ. If I did not believe that Christ overcame death on the cross and bodily rose from the grave, I would have quit preaching years ago. I am absolutely convinced that Jesus is living at this moment at the right hand of God the Father and reigns in my heart. I believe it by faith, and I believe it by evidence found in the Scriptures.

Luke, a physician and disciple of Jesus, was one of the most brilliant men of his day; he made this startling statement about the resurrection in the book of Acts: "He . . . presented Himself alive after His suffering by many infallible proofs, being seen by them during forty days and speaking of the things pertaining to the kingdom of God" (Acts 1:3).

These "infallible proofs" have been debated for two thousand years. Many people have come to know the truth while they tried to prove Jesus' resurrection a lie and failed. Others ignore the facts recorded in the best-selling book of all time, the Bible.

DEFINING HISTORY

Television and radio host Larry King, who has been a friend of mine for many years, was once asked what historical figure he would most want to interview. His answer? Jesus. "I would like to ask Him if He was indeed virgin-born. The answer to that question would define history for me."[2]

My response is always that Jesus *was* virgin born because the Bible says so. The angel appeared to Joseph and said, "Do not be afraid to take Mary home as your wife, because what is conceived in her is from the Holy Spirit. She will give birth to a son, and you are to give him the name Jesus, because he will save his people from their sins" (Matthew 1:20–21 NIV).

The virgin birth is a stumbling block for many because they refuse to believe God's Word—the Bible—as evidence. You cannot believe in someone if you do not believe their words.

Jesus was born of a virgin, fulfilling prophecy. Jesus was crucified on a cross, fulfilling prophecy. Jesus died for the sins of mankind, fulfilling prophecy. Jesus was buried in a borrowed tomb, fulfilling prophecy. Jesus was raised from the dead, fulfilling prophecy. Jesus ascended into the heavens, also fulfilling prophecy. And this same Jesus will come again one day in fulfillment of prophecy. This is the hope and certainty of all those who believe in Him.

You may say, "Well, I don't believe." I would ask you this simple question: "Why?" Many people do not believe that Jesus ever existed, much less died and rose again, yet the calendar uses the birth of Jesus as the central point of time. Why? Because He came to earth, He died and rose again, and He is coming back. Jesus *has* defined history, giving hope for our tomorrows.

While much of the world challenges those of the Christian faith to prove the actual existence of Jesus, a post on a prominent atheist website states that denying Jesus existed is like "saying . . . somebody willfully ignores the overwhelming evidence." Another says that "if he didn't exist, we'll never be able to prove it."[3]

WHY QUESTION THE FACTS?

The Old Testament predicted Christ's birth, death, and resurrection, and the New Testament documents the fulfillment of these prophecies, yet many people reject its truth. Why is it that the biographies of so many others are believed when they were written long after their deaths?

Alexander the Great's biography, for instance, was written four hundred years after he died, so its author obviously never knew him. But Alexander's legacy lives on while people doubt the life of Christ as documented by the Gospel writers who walked with Jesus.[4]

Many people down through the centuries never had a record of their own births. Yet the existence of Jesus is still called into question despite the intricate genealogy, recorded in the Bible, that has stood the test of time. Skeptics question His existence because of the "silent" years from age twelve to thirty. Yet the Bible documents great numbers of eyewitness accounts of His birth, His Person, His ministry, His death, and His bodily resurrection.

Did you know some today question whether William Shakespeare wrote the plays that bear his name? Why? Because "not one of Shakespeare's original manuscripts survives."[5] Many scholars claim that a "practical, down-to-earth rustic from the English outback . . . lacked the sophistication . . . and depth of knowledge to produce a great body of brilliant work."[6] A well-known Shakespearean actor stated in a *Washington Times* article, "I'm pretty convinced our playwright wasn't that fellow."[7]

Some see Shakespeare as a legend, a pseudonym, because there are no documents dating his birth or what Shakespeare did between the 1580s and 1592;[8] there are simply no accounts of his life during this time. His biography is peppered with suppositions and possibilities, yet "Shakespeare is the second most quoted writer in the English language— after the various writers of the Bible."[9]

Does that surprise you? It did me. Shakespeare's work is acclaimed in the literary world as genius, proving the truth of the famous eulogy by his fellow poet Ben Jonson: "He was not of an age, *but for all time!*"[10]

A very credible online article entitled "How We Know That Shakespeare Wrote Shakespeare" invites the reader to consider a number of historical facts, one being that the playwright's "contemporaries knew who he was, and there was never any doubt in the minds of those who knew him."[11] The authors conclude:

> How do we know that Shakespeare wrote Shakespeare? We know because the historical record tells us so, strongly and unequivocally. The historical evidence demonstrates that one and the same man, William Shakespeare of Stratford-upon-Avon, was . . . William Shakespeare the author of the plays and poems that bear his name. . . .
>
> [Those who assert otherwise] must rely solely upon speculation about what they think the "real" author *should* have been like, because they cannot produce one historical fact to bolster their refusal to accept who that author actually *was*. No matter how they try to ignore it or explain it away, the historical record—all of it—establishes William Shakespeare of Stratford-upon-Avon as the author of the works traditionally attributed to him.[12]

In his last will and testament, revised one month before his death, Shakespeare stated:

> In the name of God . . . I William Shakespeare of Stratford upon Avon . . . in perfect health and memory, God be praised, do make and ordain this my last will and testament in manner and form following—that is to say, first, I commend my soul into the hands of God my Creator, hoping and assuredly believing, through the merits of Jesus Christ my Saviour, to be made partaker of life everlasting.[13]

Engraved on his tombstone are these words:

> Good friend, for Jesus' sake forbear. . . .
> Blest be the man that spares these stones,
> And curst be he that moves my bones.[14]

"Though it was customary to dig up the bones from previous graves to make room for others, Shakespeare's remains are still undisturbed."[15]

I never met the great playwright, of course, but I believe he existed. His work has remained for this age, but his *remains*, by his own admission, are in the grave, awaiting the next great and monumental event of all time, the return of Jesus Christ. Jesus, not Shakespeare, is the One who is "not of an age, but for all time." Jesus Himself said: "Behold, I am coming quickly . . . I am . . . the Beginning and the End, the First and the Last" (Revelation 22:12–13).

You will never meet Shakespeare in this life because he is dead. But you can meet Jesus Christ in this life because He lives! The marks of His sacrifice on the cross are found in human hearts. Most gravestones bear the words: "Here lie the remains of . . ." But from Christ's tomb came the living words of an angel, declaring: "He is not here, but is risen!" (Luke 24:6). Jesus' tomb is history's only empty grave. Christianity has no dusty remains of the Savior to venerate, not a tomb or shrine of His to worship.

Many lawyers and jurists of history became convinced that the resurrection of Jesus Christ is a great and attested fact of history. John Singleton Copley, Lord Lyndhurst, considered one of the greatest legal minds in nineteenth-century Britain, stated it this way: "I know pretty well what evidence is; and I tell you, such evidence as that for the Resurrection [of Christ] has never broken down yet."[16]

Simon Greenleaf of Harvard University was one of "the finest writers and best esteemed legal authorities in [the nineteenth] century,"[17] and his 1842 text *A Treatise on the Law of Evidence* is still considered a classic.[18] In his book *Testimony of the Evangelists*, he approached the matter of Christ's resurrection from the standpoint of fact and evidence and concluded, "It was therefore impossible that [the Gospel writers] could have persisted in affirming the truths they have narrated, had not Jesus actually rose from the dead."[19]

Dr. William Lyon Phelps, beloved professor of English literature at

Yale University for many years, declared, "The historical evidence for the resurrection [of Christ] is stronger than any other miracle."[20]

These statements are from leading intellectuals who have studied the matter from the standpoint of valid evidence, so the voice of the scholar harmonizes with that of the angels and the disciples to declare in certainty today: "Christ the Lord is risen today."[21]

There is more evidence that Jesus rose from the dead than there is that Julius Caesar ever lived or that Alexander the Great died at the age of thirty-three. It is strange that historians will accept thousands of facts for which they can produce only shreds of evidence. But in the face of the overwhelming evidence of the resurrection of Jesus Christ, they cast a skeptical eye and hold intellectual doubts. The trouble with these people is that they do not *want* to believe. Their spiritual vision is so blinded, and they are so completely prejudiced, that they cannot accept the glorious fact of the resurrection of Christ on Bible testimony alone.

While many institutions are reluctant to authenticate biblical accounts, the Smithsonian Institution states:

> The Bible, in particular the historical books of the old testament, are as accurate historical documents as any that we have from antiquity and are in fact more accurate than many of the Egyptian, Mesopotamian, or Greek histories.
>
> These Biblical records can be and are used . . . in archeological work. For the most part, historical events described took place and the peoples cited really existed.[22]

The world of science cannot unequivocally deny the Bible, and neither can history, based on the evidence of eyewitness accounts. Here is what the Bible says:

> For I delivered to you first of all . . . that Christ died for our sins according to the Scriptures, and that He was buried, and that He rose again the third day according to the Scriptures, and that He was seen by

Cephas [Peter], then by the twelve. After that He was seen by over five hundred brethren at once, of whom the greater part remain to the present. (1 Corinthians 15:3–6)

And what about the fact that when Jesus breathed His last, there was a great earthquake and graves opened, and many dead people were raised to life? If you had been there and witnessed your loved ones walking around after you had buried them, would you believe? Would it change your life?

Satan is on the move to discredit God's Word and the resurrection. He plays with our minds, causing us to doubt, just as he did with Eve in the garden so long ago. His tactics have not changed. Jesus said, "My words will never pass away" (Luke 21:33 NIV).

There is no middle ground when it comes to Jesus Christ. You either believe Him and live for Him or reject Him and live for yourself. Satan relentlessly whispers in your ear, trying to plant doubt in your mind about the truth.

For those who have not answered the question, "Where is Jesus?" Satan wants you to reject the fact that He lives today in the hearts of those who believe in Him. For those who have settled the question, Satan wants you to doubt Christ's power in your life. It is important to know who the enemy is and how his battle plan unfolds. From the beginning Satan longed to rob God of His rightful place, His throne of glory and power. Satan will never accomplish his goal in the big picture, but he can accomplish it in our lives if we let him, instead of the resurrected Christ, rule in our hearts.

DOWN THROUGH THE CENTURIES

Jesus once asked His disciples a challenging question:

Now Jesus and His disciples went out to the towns of Caesarea Philippi; and on the road He asked His disciples, saying to them, "Who do men say that I am?"

So they answered, "John the Baptist; but some say, Elijah; and others, one of the prophets."

He said to them, "But who do you say that I am?"

Peter answered and said to Him, "You are the Christ." (Mark 8:27–29)

As you read these pages, do you sense Jesus asking, "Who do you say that I am?"

Well, it is interesting to go back through the centuries and consider what others have said about Jesus. Skeptics claim that the Scriptures are not believable, yet testimonies about Jesus' life and resurrection come from historians, philosophers, scientists, churchmen, and, yes, even atheists. Evidence is substantiated in scrolls of antiquity, quill-stained parchments, and modern communications.

Centuries of history document testimony concerning Jesus. As early as the first century, a Jewish historian named Flavius Josephus, whose personal acceptance of Jesus as Messiah is debatable, confirmed the impact Jesus Christ made in the hearts of His followers:

> About this time there lived Jesus, a wise man. . . . He won over many Jews and many of the Greeks. He was the Messiah. When Pilate . . . had condemned him to be crucified, those who had in the first place come to love him did not give up their affection for him. On the third day he appeared to them restored to life, for the prophets of God had prophesied these and countless other marvelous things about him. And the tribe of the Christians, so called after him, has still to this day not disappeared.[23]

Justin Martyr and Tertullian, second-century historians and philosophers, refer to the existence of an official document in Rome from Pontius Pilate that speaks of Jesus' crucifixion: "Tiberius . . . having himself received intelligence from Palestine of events which had clearly shown the truth of Christ's divinity, brought the matter before the senate, with his own decision in favor of Christ."[24]

In fact, the acts of Pontius Pilate related to Jesus' trial, crucifixion, and resurrection are documented by quite a few early sources, most notably Justin, Tertullian, and Eusebius, who reported on their examination of letters from Pilate to Tiberius Caesar regarding the trial and execution of Jesus.[25] While many call into question the authenticity of such resources, it is not so inconceivable to believe that the most dramatic event in Israel would not be properly documented by the ruling procurator of Judea, who would be expected to give full account to the emperor of Rome.

Even negative historical documents carry evidence of the truth and power of the biblical story. The fourth-century Roman emperor named Julian the Apostate opposed Christians and wrote of them disparagingly, but even his insults bear witness:

> Jesus . . . has now been celebrated about three hundred years having done nothing in his lifetime worthy of fame, unless anyone thinks it is a very great work to heal lame and blind people and exorcise demoniacs. . . . These impious Galileans not only feed their own poor, but ours also; welcoming them into their agapae [love].[26]

The end of Julian's life bears an interesting "backward" testimony as well. He was fatally wounded during a battle with the Persians and died sometime later. Many accounts claim that as he held up his dagger toward the sky, his last words were, "Vicisti, Galilaee," which translates, "Thou hast conquered, O Galilean."[27]

The Athenian philosopher Socrates lived four centuries before Jesus and was engaged in the pursuit of truth. His most famous quote is "I know that I know nothing."[28] Though this famous Greek left no written word behind him, we know about him because his followers, particularly Plato, "wrote their recollections of what he had said and done."[29] One writer has noted that "Socrates taught for 40 years, Plato for 50, Aristotle for 40, and Jesus for only 3. Yet the influence of Christ's 3-year ministry infinitely transcends the impact left by the combined 130 years of teaching from these men who were among the greatest philosophers of all antiquity."[30] This opinion echoes that of Augustine in the fourth century: "I have read in Plato and Cicero sayings that are very wise and very beautiful; but I never read in either of them: 'Come unto me all ye that labor and are heavy laden.'"[31]

Many centuries later, in the 1700s, the influential Swiss-French philosopher Jean Jacques Rousseau wrote admiringly of Jesus:

> If the life and death of Socrates are those of a sage, the life and death of Jesus are those of a God. Shall we suppose the evangelic history a mere fiction? . . . it bears not the marks of fiction. On the contrary, the history of Socrates, which nobody presumes to doubt, is not so well attested as that of Jesus Christ.[32]

And since the truth of Christ is absolute, His life and death confirms the fulfillment of His resurrection.

Johann Sebastian Bach's masterpieces of the eighteenth century were centered on Christ's death and resurrection. When Bach died in 1750, it was said that he "yield[ed] up his blessed soul to his saviour."[33]

The emperor Napoleon in the early nineteenth century spoke convincingly of the truth of the Bible's claims about Jesus:

> I know men, and I tell you that Jesus Christ is not a [mere] man. Superficial minds see a resemblance between Christ and the founders of empires and the gods of other religions. That resemblance does not exist. . . . I search in vain in history to find the similar to Jesus Christ, or any thing which can approach the gospel. Neither history, nor humanity, nor the ages, nor nature offer me any thing with which I am able to compare it or to explain it. Here every thing is extraordinary. The more I consider the gospel, the more I am assured that there is nothing there which is not beyond the march of events and above the human mind. . . . You speak of Caesar, of Alexander; of their conquests, and of the enthusiasm which they enkindled in the hearts

of their soldiers. But can you conceive of a dead man making conquests, with an army faithful and entirely devoted to his memory. My armies have forgotten me, even while living, as the Carthaginian army forgot Hannibal. Such is our power! . . . Alexander, Caesar, Charlemagne, and myself founded empires. But upon what did we rest the creations of our genius? Upon *force*. Jesus Christ alone founded his empire upon *love*; and at this hour millions of men would die for him.[34]

Vincent Van Gogh, the great Dutch painter and mysterious personality, commented "Christ . . . is more of an artist than the artists; he works in the living spirit and the living flesh, he makes *men* instead of statues."[35]

Lord Byron, the British Romantic poet from a generation earlier, stated even more concisely, "If ever man was God or God man, Jesus Christ was both."[36]

And classic science-fiction novelist H. G. Wells wrote in 1935:

It is interesting and significant that a historian, without any theological bias whatever, should find that he cannot portray the progress of humanity honestly without giving a foremost place to a penniless teacher from Nazareth. . . . [One] like myself, who does not even call himself a Christian, finds the picture centering irresistibly around the life and character of this most significant man. . . . the world began to be a different world from the day that [His] doctrine was preached.[37]

Why is this? Because Jesus is the Word of God in flesh. He was resurrected to fulfill that living Word, and He lives today.

The prolific and eloquent nineteenth-century novelist Charles Dickens wrote, "I now most solemnly impress upon you the truth and beauty of the Christian religion, as it came from Christ Himself."[38]

The American statesman Daniel Webster said, "If I could comprehend [Jesus Christ], he could be no greater than myself. Such is my sense of sin, and consciousness of my inability to save myself, that I feel I need a super-human Saviour."[39] A short time before he died in 1852, he wrote, "My heart has always assured and reassured me, that the Gospel of Jesus Christ must be a Divine Reality. . . . The whole history of man proves it."[40]

There is no Gospel without the certainty of the resurrection. That's what makes the Gospel the Gospel and its certain hope.

American historian George Bancroft, US secretary of the navy and founder of the US Naval Academy at Annapolis in the 1800s, said, "I find the name of Jesus Christ written on the top of every page of modern history."[41]

David Strauss, a German theologian and a most bitter opponent of the supernatural elements of the Gospels, whose work may have done more to destroy faith in Christ than the writings of any other man in modern times, confessed toward the end of his life that "This Christ . . . is *historical*, not mythical; is an individual, no mere symbol. . . . He remains the highest model of religion within the reach of our thought; and no perfect piety is possible without his presence in the heart."[42]

Swiss-born theologian and historian Philip Schaff, who wrote in response to Strauss, added this assessment:

> This Jesus of Nazareth, without money and arms, conquered more millions than Alexander, Caesar, Mohammed, and Napoleon; without science and learning, he shed more light on things human and divine than all philosophers and scholars combined; without the eloquence of schools, he spoke such words of life as were never spoken before or since, and produced effects which lie beyond the reach of any orator or poet; without writing a single line, he set more pens in motion, and furnished themes for more sermons, orations, discussions, learned volumes, works of art, and sweet songs of praise, than the whole army of great men of ancient and modern times.[43]

This man, Jesus, lived among us, died at our sinful hands, and rose from the grave to give us life everlasting.

Ernest Renan, French historian from the nineteenth century and an expert in ancient civilizations, said, . . . "all history is incomprehensible without [Christ]. . . . whatever may be the unexpected phenomena of the future, Jesus will not be surpassed. . . . all the ages will proclaim that, among the sons of men, there is none born who is greater than Jesus."[44]

Sholem Asch, a Polish-born Yiddish writer from the early twentieth century, wrote,

> Jesus Christ is to me the outstanding personality of all time, all history, both as Son of God and as Son of Man. Everything he ever said or did has value for us today and that is something you can say of no other man, dead or alive. There is no easy middle ground to stroll upon. You either accept Jesus or reject him. You can analyze Mohammed and . . . Buddha, but don't try it with him.[45]

Asch also penned this memorable line about Jesus: "He became the Light of the World. Why shouldn't I, a Jew, be proud of that?"[46]

When the Pharisees told Jesus to silence His followers for proclaiming Him the King of glory, Jesus said, "I tell you that if these should keep silent, the stones would immediately cry out" (Luke 19:40). Archaeology is a sought-after adventure. Some enter this field, studying antiquities, to disprove the Bible. But when many brush the dust of the earth from their knees, they confess that Jesus is Lord! The very rocks do cry out that Jesus lives.

Archaeologist William Albright, born in Chile of missionary parents, stated, "There can be no doubt that archaeology has confirmed the substantial historicity of Old Testament tradition."[47] Jewish archaeologist Nelson Glueck said, "It may be stated categorically that no archaeological discovery has ever controverted a Biblical reference. Scores of archaeological findings have been made which confirm in clear outline or in exact detail historical statements in the Bible."[48]

Where do you stand among these men of history when it comes to Jesus Christ?

The Jesus Effect

As communication tools became more widely available, documenting history became easier, and the twentieth century gave us libraries of information that will keep generations busy until Jesus Himself returns, confirming the overwhelming evidence found in the Bible.

Kenneth Scott Latourette, former president of the American Historical Society, stated,

> Even if we did not have the four brief accounts which we call the Gospels we could gain a fairly adequate impression of him and of the salient points of his life, teachings, death, and resurrection from references in letters of his followers written within a generation of his death. . . .
>
> It is evidence of his importance, of the effect that [Jesus] has had upon history and, presumably, of the baffling mystery of his being that no other life ever lived on this planet has evoked so huge a volume of literature among so many peoples and languages, and that, far from ebbing, the flood continues to mount . . . Some characteristics stand out so distinctly in the accounts . . . that they are a guarantee of authenticity, so obviously are they from life and not invented or even seriously distorted . . . [49]

Mahatma Gandhi of India said, "[Jesus—] a man who was completely innocent, offered himself as a sacrifice for the good of others, including his enemies, and became the ransom of the world. It was a perfect act."[50]

Orthodox Jewish scholar Pinchas Lapide said, "I accept the resurrection of Easter Sunday not as an invention of the community of disciples, but as a historical event."[51]

Dr. Charles Malik, past president of the United Nations General Assembly and someone I was privileged to know, wrote "These Things I Believe," which included this memorable line about Jesus: "His words are wonderful; his acts, including his resurrection, were wonderful; but he himself is far more wonderful. . . . he said what he said, and did what he did, only because he was who he said he was!"[52] Dr. Malik is also quoted as having asked, "Having fully realized that the whole world is dissolving before our very eyes, it is impossible to ask a more far-reaching question than this: 'Do you believe in Jesus Christ?'"[53]

Even *Newsweek* magazine editor Kenneth Woodward, with whom I have had the privilege of speaking many times, wrote at the turn of the twenty-first century and the birth of a new millennium,

> Historians did not record [Jesus'] birth. Nor, for 30 years, did anyone pay him much heed. A Jew from the Galilean hill country with a reputation for teaching and healing, he showed up at the age of 33 in Jerusalem during Passover. In three days, he was arrested, tried and convicted of treason, then executed like the commonest of criminals. His followers said that God raised him from the dead. Except among those who believed in him, the event passed without notice.
>
> Two thousand years later, the centuries themselves are measured from the birth of Jesus of Nazareth. At the end of [1999], calendars in India and China, like those in Europe, America and the Middle East, will register the dawn of the third millennium. . . . the birth of Jesus . . . number[s] the days for Christians and non-Christians alike. For Christians, Jesus is the hinge on which the door of history swings, the point at which eternity intersects with time, the Savior who redeems time by drawing all things to himself. As the second millennium draws to a close, nearly a third of the world's population claims to be his followers.[54]

Some years ago I was invited to have coffee with Konrad Adenauer before he retired as the chancellor of Germany. He asked me, "What is the most important thing in the world?" Before I could answer, he gave the right answer and said, "The resurrection of Jesus Christ. If Jesus Christ is alive, then there is hope for the world. If Jesus Christ is in the grave, then I don't see the slightest glimmer of hope on the horizon."

Legendary actor Charlton Heston recorded the famous statement, "There's been more ink—and blood—spilled over this man since they nailed Him to the cross than over any single human being in history."[55]

Even today in the twenty-first century, throngs of people acclaim the newly rediscovered Leonardo da Vinci fifteenth-century painting entitled *Savior of the World*. The piece had been lost for five hundred years, disguised by layers of overpainting, and was painstakingly restored before going on exhibit in London in 2001. When asked, "How can we know this is a da Vinci?" the answer was because art experts say so.[56]

Do great choirs and symphonies question the brilliant composer when singing or playing George Frideric Handel's *Messiah*? For more than 270 years, audiences have listened to this magnificent composition. The text for the music was compiled from the Bible by Handel's friend Charles Jennens, who chose 1 Timothy 3:16 for *Messiah's* epigraph: "God was manifested in the flesh, justified in the Spirit, seen by angels, preached among the Gentiles, believed on in the world, received up to glory."[57] When the oratorio was first performed in 1742, a member of the audience expressed gratitude to Handel for "producing such a wonderful piece of 'entertainment.' 'Entertainment!' Handel replied. 'My purpose was not to entertain, but to teach them something.'"[58] And for centuries now Handel's message has resonated in hearts, proclaiming that Jesus is the Lord who died and rose again. A soaring soprano solo in the *Messiah* masterpiece combines Job 19 and 1 Corinthians 15 to proclaim:

> I know that my Redeemer liveth . . .
> For now is Christ risen from the dead.[59]

Elvis Presley, who died in 1977, still ranks as one of America's most successful performers, filling arenas around the world via multimedia presentations. I remember seeing a clip from a concert where someone handed him a crown. Elvis stopped his song and said, "I'm not the King. There's only one King, and that's Jesus Christ." I also remember hearing international British pop icon Cliff Richard, who did a film for us some years ago, say that "no man can follow Christ and go astray."

THE LEAP OF FAITH TO ETERNAL LIFE

In October 1929, the *Saturday Evening Post* published a landmark interview with the great physicist and mathematician Albert Einstein. I find his response to questions of Jesus as a historical figure simply breathtaking. He answered, "I am a Jew, but I am enthralled by the luminous figure of the Nazarene. . . . No one can read the Gospels without feeling the actual presence of Jesus. His personality pulsates in every word. No myth is filled with such life."[60]

While no one knows if Einstein ever made Jesus the Lord of his life, he did say this near the end of his life:

> If you ask me to prove what I believe, I can't. . . . The mind can proceed only so far upon what it knows and can prove. There comes a point where the mind takes a leap . . . and comes out upon a higher plane of knowledge, but can never prove how it got there. All great discoveries have involved such a leap.[61]

This, my friend, may be the point in time for your higher plane— relying on more than others' testimonies and completely on faith in God alone because of what He says about Himself. "Most assuredly, I say to you, before Abraham was, I AM" (John 8:58). This leap of faith is given when you speak the name of Jesus in sincere truth, realizing that you are Hellbound without His forgiving grace and mercy. Ask Him to look into your barren heart and your hungry soul and fill it with the faith to believe that He will change you. No matter how much knowledge you gather, no matter how much proof you accumulate, you will never know the Lord Jesus Christ without taking the certain leap of faith that salvation comes only from Him. "Now faith is confidence in what we hope for and assurance about what we do not see. This is what the ancients were commended for" (Hebrews 11:1–2 NIV).

The question remains: What have you decided about Jesus Christ? There is no such thing as staying neutral. Peter Larson wrote, "Despite our efforts to keep Him out, God intrudes. The life of Jesus is bracketed by two impossibilities: a virgin's womb and an empty tomb.'"[62]

There are many among us today who acknowledge Jesus as a historical figure. Many even claim to follow Him, but their lives do not reflect a change in their thinking or in their behavior or whether the Holy Spirit reigns within them, enabling them to think godly thoughts and behave in a way that honors the Lord. The Bible says, "If we say that we have fellowship with Him, and walk in darkness, we lie and do not practice the truth" (1 John 1:6).

Someone wrote,

Buddha never claimed to be God. Moses never claimed to be Jehovah. Mohammed never claimed to be Allah. Yet Jesus Christ claimed to be the true and living God. Buddha simply said, "I am a teacher in search of the truth." Jesus said, "I am the Truth." Confucius said, "I never claimed to be holy." Jesus said, "Who convicts me of sin?" Mohammed said, "Unless God throws his cloak over me, I have no hope." Jesus said, "Unless you believe in me, you will die in your sins."[63]

Many years ago I visited an old monastery in India. I saw old relics that had been dug up and are now worshiped by Buddhists in the area. Muslims point with pride to Mecca, where the body of their prophet, Mohammed, is buried. Followers of Confucius revere the remains of their master, who is buried in an imposing tomb at Shandong, in the People's Republic of China. But what distinguishes Christianity from all other religions is the fact that Jesus lives and reigns as the only Savior of the world.

What do Socrates, Bach, and Shakespeare have in common? They are remembered as bigger than life, but they are dead and in the grave and can do nothing for you. Walk into the great cathedrals whose spires pierce the sky, and you will see paintings and sculptures memorializing robust men who are still revered and kind women who reached down to the lowly in compassion. But they, too, lie silent in death; they can do nothing for you.

But where is Jesus? Sadly, artists too often have depicted Him as feeble, weak, and dead—still hanging on the cross. This is not the truth; for the One who is depicted hanging lifeless and broken on the cross is instead full of the breath of life, full of glory. He drank the cup of sin for all by emptying His life's blood so that He could fill us with the gift of eternal life by His resurrection.

Look to others and see that they are no different from you and me—we don't need a religion; we need a Savior. Christianity is the faith of the empty tomb, a religion centered not on a dead leader but on the living Lord.

Proof Comes by Faith

While it is captivating to read what others say about Jesus Christ, faith is still the key to believing in Christ, who saves the sinner's soul.

As I meditate on the infallible proofs from Scripture of the life, death, and resurrection of this One solitary life, it occurs to me that there is a tremendous amount of convincing evidence—evidence that would be acceptable in any court of law as to the validity of Christ's resurrection. But there are many who still have serious doubts. I am not presumptuous when I say that I have no doubts. I have experienced the living Christ in my heart. But for some of you who may be skeptical, there are many other reasons why I am sure that Christ rose from the dead.

Christ's birth was no ordinary birth. It was accompanied by angels' voices and celestial wonders. His life was no ordinary life, for it was marked by many signs and miracles. We've seen that His death was no ordinary death, for it was distinguished by unusual compassion, geological disturbances, and solar irregularities. Such a life could not long be contained in a grave, even though it was sealed in a prison of stone.

Yes, the Old Testament predicted that Christ would rise again. Every important event in Jesus' life was described many centuries before He came in the flesh, and when Jesus came, He fulfilled every prophecy.

"The Lord Himself will give you a sign: Behold, the virgin shall conceive and bear a Son, and shall call His name Immanuel" (Isaiah 7:14). The Bible also says:

> He bore the sin of many,
> And made intercession for the transgressors.
>
> (ISAIAH 53:12)

> The LORD makes his life an offering for sin. . . .
> After the suffering of his soul,
> he will see the light of life.
>
> (ISAIAH 53:10–11 NIV)

We've also seen that during Christ's ministry He taught that He would die and be resurrected (Matthew 20:18–19). This blessed Christ, who never deviated from the truth, can certainly be trusted, and His own words comprise some of the most reliable and convincing evidence of His resurrection.

Jesus connected His own resurrection with our endless life when He said, "I am the resurrection and the life. He who believes in Me, though he may die, he shall live. And whoever lives and believes in Me shall never die" (John 11:25–26).

Do you accept these words of Jesus? I do. Even His most avowed enemies never caught Him in a lie. He, who was truth itself, can be trusted implicitly. He said He would be in the grave three days—and He was. He said He would come forth from the grave—and He did. He said that all those who believe in Him would have hope of everlasting life—and they have. He said, "I am He who lives, and was dead, and behold, I am alive forevermore" (Revelation 1:18). And we, also, will one day die and be resurrected. This is the great hope and certainty for those who follow Jesus.

We have the documented testimonies of those who were eyewitnesses to His resurrection. Angels, His disciples, the Roman soldiers, and a myriad of witnesses all shouted, "He is risen! . . . Surely He is the Son of God."

The angel said to those who came to pay tribute to the dead, "Why do you look for the living among the dead? He is not here; he has risen! Remember how he told you, while he was still with you" (Luke 24:5–6 NIV). Mary Magdalene, scarlet sinner saved by grace, rushed breathlessly to the disheartened disciples with the glad news, "I have seen the Lord!" (John 20:18 NIV).

Peter, always the outspoken one, said, "We are witnesses of everything he did in the country of the Jews and in Jerusalem. They killed him by hanging him on a cross, but God raised him from the dead on the third day and caused him to be seen. . . . by us who ate and drank with him after he rose from the dead" (Acts 10:39–41 NIV).

Peter also wrote,

> We did not follow cleverly devised stories when we told you about the coming of our Lord Jesus Christ in power, but we were eyewitnesses of his majesty. He received honor and glory from God the Father when the voice came to him from the Majestic Glory, saying, "This is my Son, whom I love; with him I am well pleased." We ourselves heard this voice that came from heaven when we were with him on the sacred mountain. (2 Peter 1:16–18 NIV)

The Bible says the apostle Paul "went into the synagogue, and on three Sabbath days he reasoned with them from the Scriptures, explaining and proving that the Messiah had to suffer and rise from the dead. 'This Jesus I am proclaiming to you is the [Christ],' he said" (Acts 17:2–3 NIV).

When you look for Jesus you will not find Him on the cross nor will you find Him in the tomb—the cross is barren, the tomb empty. Your empty heart, though, can be filled with the forgiveness of the blood-stained cross and glory of the vacant tomb. He lives and abides within those who believe and obey Him by following His Word. We live and die, and in between we are all given the same choice—what will we do with Jesus—the resurrected Christ?

Even without these proofs I would still know that Christ lives because He lives in me. I talk to Him every morning when I wake up. He walks with me, and even as I write these words, His presence is overwhelmingly known. "For I am not ashamed of the gospel of Christ, for it is the power of God to salvation for everyone who believes" (Romans 1:16).

Are you looking for Jesus? He is near you today. Look at the cross, and you will see the evidence—His blood shed for you—but He is not there. Look at the tomb, and you will see the evidence—it is empty—for He lives! The Bible says, "Look to Me, and be saved. . . . For I am God, and there is no other" (Isaiah 45:22). Look for Jesus—He is knocking at the door of your heart.

Listen to God's promise to you: "But if the Spirit of Him who raised Jesus from the dead dwells in you, He who raised Christ from the dead will also give life to your mortal bodies through His Spirit who dwells in you" (Romans 8:11). The evidence is before you. Examine it and then examine your heart. Roll back the stone of unbelief and behold the glow of an empty tomb and the thrill of a full heart and new life. The stone at Christ's tomb was not rolled away to let out Jesus but to let in the eyewitnesses to declare, "He is risen!"

James Hastings, a Scottish minister and biblical scholar in the early twentieth century, told an intriguing story about a German artist named Sternberg. As a little gypsy girl was sitting for a portrait in his studio, she noticed on the wall a half-finished portrait of Christ on the cross. The girl asked who it was. When told it was Jesus, she responded that he must have been a very wicked man to have been nailed to a cross. The painter told her that, on the contrary, "Christ was the best man that ever lived, and that He died on the cross that others might live." Then the little gypsy girl looked at him with such innocence and asked, "Did He die for you?" The question haunted Sternberg's conscience day and night, for though he knew the truth about Christ, he had not accepted Him as his Savior. He found he was no longer satisfied with life until he answered the question that you must also answer: Did He die for you?[64] If so, then you must die to self and find life anew in the resurrected Savior.

Have you received the living Christ? I am not asking you to receive a Christ who is hanging dead on a cross. Take Christ into your life—the resurrected Christ, who walks with those He has transformed by His grace. This Christ lives and is coming back to earth someday.

ARE YOU LOOKING FOR HIM? HAS HE CHANGED YOUR LIFE?

In his great mercy he has given us new birth into a living hope through the resurrection of Jesus Christ from the dead. . . . who through faith are shielded by God's power until the coming of the salvation that is ready to be revealed.

(1 PETER 1:3-5 NIV)

CHAPTER SIX

DEFINING CHRISTIANITY IN A DESIGNER WORLD

We do not belong to the night or to the darkness. . . .
But since we belong to the day, let us . . . [put] on
faith and love . . . and the hope of salvation.

—1 THESSALONIANS 5:5, 8 NIV

D O YOU LIVE IN A WORLD ALL YOUR OWN? Society today reflects the culture's craving for a designer world, one that suits every whim. We want things to go our way, according to our timeline, and at the pace of our own choosing. We want designer clothes, designer technology, designer homes and cars, even designer religion. We want either to simply belong to something or to belong to our own way. This is why so many seek to join the *right* clubs, gangs, or even churches.

Some time ago I spoke at Harvard University, and while visiting with the president, I asked him, "What appears to be the thing that young people are looking for the most?"

Without hesitation he answered, "They want to belong."

How coincidental that Facebook, a twenty-first-century phenomenon, was conceived and given birth at Harvard. This social media networking website tapped in to the deepest of human need—to belong. In October 2012, *Forbes* reported Facebook had topped a billion users—one out of every seven people on planet Earth.[1] One blogger stated that people's obsession with Facebook lies in the "innate human drive for social acceptance," which is "as old as human history."[2]

The most popular feature is that it allows individuals to include or exclude friends, creating competition for popularity by befriending or defriending people they don't even know. Facebook also gives members bragging rights to post how many friends a member has, and the most brutal is when a member's Facebook page has "0 friends."

Reuters reported that a young couple was murdered in their home by someone they had "defriended." The murderer apparently could not bear the stigma of not belonging.[3]

Social media has become something like a personal billboard, where the most intimate thoughts are posted on a wall in cyberspace. Much of the messaging flashes with frustration like neon signs. One woman blogged,

> I longed to belong. . . .
>
> So, I embarked on a journey that involved serious soul searching. . . .
>
> When we belong to a family, we practice its lifestyle. When we belong to a culture, we abide by its norms. When we belong to a religion, we follow its calling. When we belong to an organization, we conform [to] its protocols. We try to fit in.[4]

In another post she wrote:

> I realized that the only life I belonged in was my *own* . . .
>
> So, I set about creating it for myself. . . .
>
> My life was custom-built for me. And I fit perfectly in it.[5]

If that young woman is honest, she will one day post what King Solomon did in the ancient book of folly and wisdom:

> I denied myself nothing my eyes desired;
> I refused my heart no pleasure.
> My heart took delight in all my labor,
> and this was the reward for all my toil.
> Yet when I surveyed all that my hands had done
> and what I had toiled to achieve,
> everything was meaningless, a chasing after the wind;
> nothing was gained under the sun.
>
> (ECCLESIASTES 2:10–11 NIV)

The human race has always been on a quest for truth and acceptance, yet men and women are unwilling to accept the One who is the truth. His name is Almighty God, wonderful Counselor, Prince of Peace. Jesus is willing to accept all who come to Him in truth, but the world doesn't want to belong to Him.

USA Today recently featured a story about young adults and their changing attitudes about faith: "Young adults appear largely uninterested in . . . 'correct' doctrine. . . . Their God is a big God who is unbound by Scripture. . . . Clergy are seeing less emphasis on believing and more emphasis on belonging."[6]

A steady decline in "the popularity of traditional Christianity . . . in England" has prompted advertising agencies to suggest "that the Church of England try promoting itself as a trendy place to meet other people."[7] But the head of a theological think-tank told the British Broadcasting Corporation (BBC) that "the [advertising] campaigns were pushing 'designer religion,' turning worship into just another consumer item . . . 'putting the Church on the shelf next to the new cosmetic, or in the car showroom, as something to be bought.'"[8]

A similar news story in the United States, "More Americans Tailoring Religion to Fit Their Needs," states: "The folks who make up God as they go are side-by-side with self-proclaimed believers who claim the Christian label but shed their ties to traditional beliefs and practices."[9]

A leading research guru gave his findings: "People say, 'I believe in God. I believe the Bible is a good book. And then I believe whatever I want.'"[10] In the case of America, our country is moving in the direction of "310 million people with 310 million religions."[11] Professing faith in Christ is clearly not the same as *possessing* Christ, who is the source of faith.

"Whatever" has become a mantra for many, a trendy approach to a religion of belonging to self. In January 2012, *Asheville Citizen-Times* featured an article entitled "God, religion, atheism; 'So What?'" In it one young man had signed up for online dating and answered the question about religion by calling himself "spiritually apathetic." Others simply "shrug off God, religion, heaven or the ever-trendy search-for-meaning and/or purpose. Their attitude could be summed up as 'So what?' . . . Instead of followers of Jesus, they're followers of 5,000 unseen 'friends' on Facebook or Twitter."[12]

One woman tried out several Protestant denominations and finally settled on her own religion—a mix of the Baha'i and Native American traditional healing practices—while still claiming to be a Christian. She said, "I support people who do good wherever they are."[13]

After the Jewish magazine *Moment* ran a headline asking "Can There Be Judaism Without God?" publisher Nadine Epstein reported that "Most say yes. It's incredibly exciting."[14]

Prominent sociologist Robert Bellah has written about a woman named Sheila who takes the "so what" approach to a whole new level. "I can't remember the last time I went to church," she says. "My faith has carried me a long way. It's Sheilaism. Just my own little voice. . . . It's just try to love yourself and be gentle with yourself."[15]

Bellah adds Sheila is not alone: "Just because people showed up in church didn't always mean a deep personal conviction or commitment."[16]

Instead, designer religion is becoming what is known as the "one-person-one-religion trend."[17] And a Harvard psychologist once said,

"We're becoming a nation of the uncommitted,"[18] which gives insight into why there is a spirit of hopelessness in the world.

A TRENDY FAITH

As 2012 began, Microsoft reported that its Windows Design Team was working on "How to Redesign a Religion."[19] Advertising agencies are expanding their advisory capacity by offering consulting services on how to brand religion. And many churches of all persuasions are hiring research agencies to poll neighborhoods, asking what kind of church they prefer; then the local churches design themselves to fit the desires of the people. True faith in God that demands selflessness is being replaced by trendy religion that serves the selfish.

Facebook helps connect users to a site known as Religion of Individualism, where individuals can customize their own belief style to accommodate and justify how they want to live.[20] British comedian Stephen Harvey targeted this trend in a short film called "How to Start a Religion."[21]

A religion designed to reflect one's personal desire is contrary to having a personal relationship with God, who puts within His true follower His desires. Kristin Chenoweth, Tony Award–winner for the Broadway play *Wicked*, said, "I'm an actress and a singer and I'm also a Christian. . . . I just want to be like Jesus, forgiving and loving and nonjudgmental, accepting of everyone even if they don't agree."[22]

The Gospel of Jesus Christ has been watered down to a myth, causing young and old to doubt the authority of Scripture. Why is this? What is happening? God is viewed as less than the God of the Bible. Society is doing a good job of convincing the world that Jesus has no power to judge sin. Some believe that following His example of doing good to others is what empowers us to be good.

Our world does not object to this kind of Christianity—content to have only a social Christ who provides what we want for ourselves. There are those who would keep Him dying, bleeding, and incapacitated, a Christ who doesn't come down and smash the falseness of their ideologies.

What the world does object to is a living Christ, a risen Christ who is all-knowing and all-powerful. People in general do not want to meet the moral conditions that Jesus Christ demands. So we try to rationalize away the fullness of Christ, which includes His resurrection and His demand that those who follow Him live in obedience to His Word.

One young woman spoke for her generation, "We live in a cruel world, so we only go to churches that make us feel good about ourselves."

"Getting in touch with myself," a young man bragged, "is true spiritualism."

Such attitudes of self-worship are nothing new. You may be told that this form of religion is revolutionary, but the Bible says, "Woe to those who are wise in their own eyes and clever in their own sight" (Isaiah 5:21 NIV). Society may think itself clever in devising new ways and new things to worship, but the Bible tells us that "there is nothing new under the sun" (Ecclesiastes 1:9).

Jesus indicated that there would be a permissive society right before He comes back. And the world seems to be on an immoral binge such as has not been known since the days of ancient Rome. We live in a hedonistic society, and what we are seeing is human nature expressing itself without God.

People are hiring life coaches to help them get "in touch with self." A popular life-coach site claims to successfully get clients grounded spiritually, yet there is no sign of biblical authority, just personal experience extracted from the idea that if you "do for others and yourself," you will discover personal satisfaction. The Bible warns against such thinking: "For certain individuals whose condemnation was written about long ago have secretly slipped in among you. They are ungodly people, who pervert the grace of our God into a license for immorality and deny Jesus Christ our only Sovereign and Lord" (Jude 4 NIV).

In designer religions social awareness has replaced the Spirit-filled life. The truth is people would rather put their energies into "working for God" than actively "believing in God" and obeying Him. There is a difference. Busyness is the devil's playground. If we do not believe in Him and give Him the priority in our lives, working for Him is a futile exercise—because Jesus said, "Without Me you can do nothing" (John 15:5).

What some think is a new idea is as old as the Bible itself. Jeroboam, the king of northern Israel, built temples in high places for the people to worship many gods, and "this thing became a sin; the people came to worship the one at Bethel and went as far as Dan to worship the other" (1 Kings 12:30 NIV). In other words, the people continued worshiping God and also worshiping the golden calves that the king had set in place, a practice clearly forbidden by the first commandment to have no other gods but the one true God.

FAITH BLENDING

This is what is taking place in the twenty-first century—mixing claims of faith in God while worshiping other gods.

Religion is being rebranded as spiritualism and encompasses *whatever* it is people want to put their energies into, as long as it is cloaked with tolerance.

We see Coexist bumper stickers plastered on vehicles, hung in store windows, and pasted across the foreheads of rock stars. The Coexist movement is branded by spelling its name with the symbols of Islam, peace, gender, Judaism, Wicca/Paganism/Baha'i, Taoism/Confucianism, and Christianity. It is considered design history for religious tolerance.[23] There is also a movement called "Chrislam," blending Christianity with Islam and claiming that the differences should be overlooked in the spirit of unity.[24]

Actress Sharon Stone, an Oscar nominee and Golden Globe winner, considers herself a Buddhist, but "nonetheless claims an abiding belief in a traditional God."[25]

One news writer reported the following:

> Today's Christian hipsters retain their faith, but they want it to be compatible with, not contrary to, secular hipster counterculture. Their mission is to rebrand Christianity to be, if not completely void of its own brand altogether, at least cobranded and allied with the things that it had previously set itself in opposition to. . . .
>
> As a result of its intentional melding of Christian and secular . . . one cannot easily decipher the [difference].[26]

Newsweek magazine reported in 2009 that "the rising numbers of religiously unaffiliated . . . are people more apt to call themselves 'spiritual' rather than 'religious.'"[27] In the years since that article appeared, the trend continues.

BELONGING TO A DESIGNER WORLD

In the first decade of the twenty-first century the BBC ran a television series entitled *Belonging*, about a family who encountered the trials and tribulations in the changing environment of their South Wales town as they struggled to belong to an altered society.[28]

Hollywood actor James Caan rightly pointed out that "a sense of belonging is a big thing today."[29] Yet we live in a cyberspace world, where many people feel more at ease staring into the electronic face of a device than into human eyes, much less "the eyes of the LORD [that] search the whole earth" (2 Chronicles 16:9 NLT).

The word *belonging* is an endearing term in our designer society. A self-appointed pop culture philosopher wrote:

> We are all longing to go home to some place we have never been. . . . Somewhere a circle of hands will open to receive us, eyes will light up as we enter, voices will celebrate with us whenever we come into our

own power. Community means . . . arms to hold us when we falter. A circle of healing. A circle of friends. Someplace where we can be free.[30]

This is Heaven to her, but I would ask, "If she puts confidence in her own power, why does she need arms to hold her when she falters?" She cannot identify that "someplace" because when people operate out of their own feeble and powerless resource, it only leads to the place of defeat.

She is searching for God but in all the wrong places. Many others like her are in distress, refusing to submit to God who created them, exchanging God's standard for alternative lifestyles that are not ordained by God, who is the very source of life.

The very first institution that God gave mankind is also under attack as same-sex marriage is being acclaimed. Families are fractured with single-parent homes on the rise. Acceptable now is the phenomenon of men and women living together outside of marriage while others look the other way. The parents of such a couple excused this behavior with sighs of relief that "at least they're male and female living together" (and not in homosexual partnerships).

In fall of 2012, CNN Headline News carried a story about a woman who married herself, reciting the vow "with this ring I *me* wed," giving herself a new name: "Only." She spoke of the vow of self-commitment in her self-marriage that would provide her self-bliss.[31] And this is not an isolated story. In May, another woman had exchanged rings with her inner groom, vowing, "I, Nadine, promise to enjoy inhabiting my own life and to relish in a lifelong love affair with my beautiful self."[32] When asked by CNN's Anderson Cooper why she did this, she answered, "I started discovering that the love I need, it's in here" [she pointed to her heart]. After a man was married to himself for a few years, he divorced himself, claiming irreconcilable differences, and said he would look for happiness somewhere else and a place to belong.[33]

In the 2011 primary election, my home state of North Carolina actually placed an amendment on the ballot to define marriage. I never thought we would have to debate the definition of marriage, something that God has clearly ordained as a sacred union between a man and woman. Nearly every major television network has incorporated programs into primetime viewing that promote homosexuality. Books such as *My Two Moms* highlight the fact that same-sex parenting is becoming an acceptable norm.[34]

In summer of 2011, Dan Cathy, CEO of Chick-fil-a, was assaulted in the press and by the public for daring to answer a question in support of God's definition of marriage.[35] I have known Dan's father, Truett Cathy, founder of the popular restaurant chain, for many years, and I find it astounding to think that a movement would come against this Christian family for standing up for their moral values while popular media applaud immorality, spoof family values, and celebrate divorce, including on television programs such as *Happily Divorced*.

A brand-new business has opened in the Netherlands, called Heartbreak Hotel, but it's not an actual hotel. It is a marketing package tailored to couples seeking divorce. The company discreetly puts them up in one of several hotels. They check in on Friday night as married couples, meet with relationship counselors and attorneys, sign documents during the weekend, and then check out Sunday morning as singles.[36]

Even as I write this chapter, network news is reporting on the gripping reality of gendercide—a form of abortion that applies a standard of systematic extermination to a particular gender, usually girls. The traditional preference for boys in many cultures has combined with the trend for smaller families and the ability to determine the sex of a child while still in the womb. This practice has led to a serious imbalance of the sexes in China and North India.[37] And in spring of 2012, this procedure was actually being debated in the United States Congress, with strong support for allowing parents to rob the innocent of their right to life because they happen to be the wrong gender.[38]

We have dismissed God, resulting in skewed thinking and consciences that are desensitized to right and wrong, and base moral decisions solely on what "fits in" with our individual preferences.

Occupy Wall Street, a protest that began in September 2011, is self-described as a "people-powered movement"[39] and really involves giving all the "occupiers" the opportunity to freely access whatever it is they want. People expecting to have the finest of everything without working for it—this is the designer world thought up by mankind's total depravity that fails to bring contentment. In fact, the more we have, the more we want.

Many believe that pagan worship is a thing of the past, but it is ever present—we have just given it a new name: pop culture designed to satisfy self. Our self-designed world will face Almighty God someday. He has designed a particular time to meet each individual one-on-one, and we will all give account for our lives. God in His graciousness has given mankind ample notice:

> And He has made from one blood every nation of men to dwell on all the face of the earth, and has determined their preappointed times and the boundaries of their dwellings, so that they should seek the Lord . . . and find Him, though He is not far from each one of us; for in Him we live and move and have our being. . . . Now [God] commands all [people] everywhere to repent, because He has appointed a day on which He will judge the world in righteousness by the Man whom He has ordained. He has given assurance of this to all by raising Him from the dead. (Acts 17:26–28, 30–31)

That Man is the Lord Jesus.

One day we all will see what the pop culture philosopher says she longs for—true belonging—but it will not be a circle of hands that welcomes us into that Someplace. We will instead meet God on His terms, on His turf, and in His way. We will behold the nail-scarred hands of God's Son that bear the marks of our sin. We will gaze into His eyes, which can see into our very souls. We will hear the voice of God pronounce a blessing

THE REASON FOR MY HOPE

or a curse and, in that day, we will be powerless to choose. Some will be welcomed into His arms, and others will be condemned to the never-ending distance that separates them from the eternal circle of fellowship around His Heavenly throne. We will know freedom from sin, or we will be cast into the everlasting bondage that we chose while on earth.

Do you belong to the designer world of futility or to "the Way" of faith (Acts 24:14), the eternal world that God has designed for all who live according to His truth?

SEARCHING SOULS

Pop culture is searching, perhaps today more than ever, for truth. But truth has become to many *whatever* they want it to be, bound up in lies from Satan that cause them to look in futility to others and, sometimes, to themselves. Rock star Jewel sings about being God's eyes, God's hands, God's mind, God's heart.[40] While those who follow Christ may perform good deeds in His name, humanity will never be God's eyes or God's mind. Only His eyes can peer into our weary souls. He says, "For My thoughts are not your thoughts, nor are your ways My ways" (Isaiah 55:8). God longs to fill our minds with His truth and heal our sick hearts. God's heart's desire is to love us and change us.

I was moved when I heard the story that at age sixteen Jewel was traveling through Mexico and observed that everyone seemed to be looking "for someone to save them."[41] Her evaluation was true. She later wrote lyrics to what would become a major hit, "Who Will Save Your Soul?" in which she reveals people's worry about who will save their souls.[42]

I wish I could tell this talented young entertainer who is searching for God that humanity is not God and never will be. And aren't we glad? No one cares for us as God does, and no one but God loves us with an everlasting love.

The world would have us believe that we do not have souls or that we are our own gods. *The Huffington Post*'s article on "25 Ways to Feed

Your Soul"[43] was really all about pampering self. Yet the world applauds the poets who have written about searching the soul and artists who have attempted to depict the depth of the soul.

Canadian writer Douglas Coupland tapped in to our cultural soul-confusion in a poignant line by a character in his novel *The Gum Thief*: "I don't deserve a soul, yet I still have one. I know because it hurts."[44] So many men, women, and children in our society know that ache. How I hope they hear the message that can bring comfort to their aching souls. The apostle Paul wrote, "Now may the God of peace Himself sanctify you completely . . . your whole spirit, soul, and body" (1 Thessalonians 5:23).

Tormented poet Sylvia Plath famously wrote that she was terrified by a "dark thing" inside her.[45] When the soul is separated from the God who made it, the soul is indeed dark. Edgar Allan Poe said when he was dying, "Lord help my poor soul."[46] It is said that this brilliant poet lived in a great neurotic darkness. But Jesus said, "I am the light of the world. He who follows Me shall not walk in darkness, but have the light of life" (John 8:12).

Matchmaking has become a booming business from Africa to Asia, from Australia to Europe, in our culture's restless search for a "soul mate." Online services promise to bring light into your life by matching you up with someone just right for you. "Relationship experts" teach clients to practice "self-love" in order to attract a potential partner. One such expert wrote, "We . . . have the power to create our own personal movie-like narratives, love stories based on our own desires and hopes."[47]

Since the subject of the soul has a prominent place in our thinking, may I ask: Have you found the *sole* source of the real kind of love that can bring light into your life? Salvation in Jesus Christ is the only hope for your soul. Only He can illumine the dark corners of your life and give you soul satisfaction. You can continue searching for some religion that fits your particular lifestyle, but your search will never come to a satisfying end. Or you can commit your life completely to the Lord, who brings true and lasting fulfillment to the human soul who sincerely seeks Him in truth.

You can belong to the Giver of life who saves souls from the weariness of manmade religion. You can have a personal relationship with Jesus Christ. That's what it means to be a Christian. Have you humbled yourself before Him?

No Religion Can Save

Perhaps your answer is, "I think so." That answer will not bring peace to your soul. Nor will it enable you to walk in the power of knowing that Jesus Christ lives within you through His Holy Spirit, guiding you through the trials and tribulations of life that will surely come.

No religion will save your soul because religion did not die to redeem your soul. Only the Man Jesus Christ, the Son of God, died in order that your soul might live. And those whose souls bear the conviction of sin, guilt, and shame and who confess their need to holy God will receive the gift of salvation through redemption in Jesus Christ.

True Christianity is not religion. True Christianity is faith in Christ alone.

Just because people claim to be Christian does not necessarily mean that they are Christian. Christianity is not something you add to your life. Becoming a Christian means that Jesus Christ comes into your life and takes over. It is a totally new outlook that is not satisfied with anything less than penetration into the furthest corners of the soul and the understanding.

Christianity is not a spectator sport—buying a ticket and sitting on the sidelines. Becoming a Christian means no longer living for yourself but for God in obedience to Him. You must leave the old life behind and step into a new way of living, where Christ makes possible what you think impossible. To say you believe in Him and then continue living as though nothing has changed is to deny the power of God in your new life.

You cannot have Jesus in your life without change. Jesus is not an add-on. He is the Advocate to the soul who is willing to set self aside and let Jesus Christ reside within. The Bible says, "If anyone is in Christ, he is a new creation; old things have passed away; behold, all things have become new" (2 Corinthians 5:17).

How does this happen? Christ indwells His followers by giving the gift of His Holy Spirit. He will not muscle His way in; you must invite Him in, accept His gift, knowing that He will never leave. The Holy Spirit then becomes your constant companion, a lifetime resident, One who will "never leave you nor forsake you" (Hebrews 13:5). He gives you the power to begin thinking new thoughts and behaving in ways that please Him—not yourself.

The Bible says, "Put on the new man who is renewed in knowledge according to the image of Him who created him" (Colossians 3:10). That is what it means to invite Jesus into your life.

He is not going to come in and ignore the chains that bind you to sin. He is not going to come in and close His eyes to the immorality that governs your relationships. He is not going to come in and overlook your indifference to His commands. He is going to mold you and make you new by changing your very nature.

BORN TO CRAWL, REBORN TO FLY

Perhaps you are saying, "That is impossible!" That is what the caterpillar might say to a butterfly. But the same God who transforms the caterpillar into a butterfly can also change you.

Who would ever look at a caterpillar inching on its belly in the dirt and think that within a short time it would be transformed into a flying wonder? Let's look at the nature of caterpillars. Some are poisonous and capable of spewing acid. They are colored to resemble the plants on which they feed and often mimic plant parts, such as thorns. Some caterpillars are unaffected by the poison they consume from the toxic plants they feed on. And caterpillars can be a nuisance, harming the growth of food-producing plants.

When it is time for the caterpillar to transform, it attaches itself firmly to a stem or branch and forms a chrysalis or spins a cocoon for protection. Then it waits—usually for months. While it appears motionless on the outside, a tremendous amount of activity is taking place inside. The caterpillar's anatomy is miraculously disassembled and reconstructed. Wings form and absorb a great deal of nutrients, preparing for the day their veins will engorge with blood, stretch out, and fly. No doubt its view of the world will be quite different in the air than from the ground. From a slithering and destructive insect emerges a magnificent creature, feeding on the sweet nectar of the flowers. The beauty the butterfly adds to nature is intriguing as their wings absorb, reflect, and scatter light. The caterpillar is born to crawl, but it is reborn to fly.

What a picture God has given us from nature. It is interesting that the ancient Greek word for butterfly is *psyche*, meaning the very life of the soul. The caterpillar's transformation is a wonderfully symbolic picture of the miracle work of Christ in transforming a lost soul into a vibrant believer. The metamorphosis is a recurring miracle that He masterfully accomplishes in those who entrust their lives to the One who does His transforming work.

Lost souls feed on the toxins of sin. Many are immune to the poison and unable to notice the damage that has taken place in their souls. But when lost souls find salvation in Jesus Christ, they attach themselves firmly to Him. They feed on the nutrients of His Word and emerge as new creations. The blood of the Savior cleanses their dirty souls, which have groveled around in sin, and His life-giving blood infuses them with His light-giving nature. He lifts them up out of the darkened path and points them to a better way—scattering His light into the dark world from which they came. This is what it means to be a Christian. Have you experienced this transforming miracle? To be a Christian, one is born anew. This is why Jesus said, "I tell you the truth, unless you are born again, you cannot see the Kingdom of God" (John 3:3 NLT).

Jesus often used nature to illustrate His truth, and one of His most powerful illustrations involved a vine and its branches. He said, "I am the true vine. . . . You are already clean because of the word which I have spoken to you. Abide in Me, and I in you. As the branch cannot bear fruit of itself, unless it abides in the vine, neither can you, unless you abide in Me. I am the vine, you are the branches" (John 15:1, 3–5).

The analogy is clear. Christians draw holy strength from the vine that makes holy living possible. You may say that it seems a little egotistical to claim to be holy. But read carefully what the Bible says: "As obedient children, do not conform to the evil desires you had when you lived in ignorance. But just as he who called you is holy, so be holy in all you do; for it is written: 'Be holy, because I am holy'" (1 Peter 1:14–16 NIV).

When Christ transforms us into new creations we have new positions in Him, and He helps us to reflect the holiness of His character. The Bible says, "Your body is the temple of the Holy Spirit who is in you" (1 Corinthians 6:19).

Living a holy life means that you give yourself wholly to Christ. That doesn't mean you will be perfect, for perfection in Christ will be a Heavenly transaction. But if you do not desire to live according to the ways of God, your longing for salvation is insincere. If the cross of Christ has not changed you, then you are not following Him.

You may ask, "Will the world think I am strange if I commit my life to Him?" Probably. But stranger is the fact that while the world accepts enthusiasm in every realm of life but the spiritual, the world does expect Christians to look different, talk differently, and act differently.

I'M A CHRISTIAN BECAUSE . . .

There is great confusion today in what it means to be a Christian. It is frequently debated in news forums on network television and on the Internet. Many think that going to church makes them a Christian, especially those who belong to a particular church. Others say that they are Christians because they believe in Jesus Christ. Some say they are Christians because they pray and read the Bible. Multitudes believe that going to confession makes them a Christian, while others believe they are Christians because they were born into a Christian home.

Then there are those who believe they are Christians because they give to organizations that feed the poor or go on mission trips to help build houses for the homeless or give medicine to the sick. Some believe they are Christians because they deny themselves sinful pleasures. Many people believe they are Christians because they try to love their neighbors. Many others believe that because they prayed a prayer they are Christians. People say they are Christians because they follow Jesus' example of loving their enemies, and others claim Christianity because they have faith that Jesus will grant them their desires.

Do you fit into one or more of these categories? Do you really understand what it means to belong to Jesus? How many know beyond a shadow of doubt that they are a Christian and truly follow Him?

You see, the issue is not "What does becoming a Christian mean to you?" but "What did Jesus say about becoming one of His followers?" The Bible says,

> He who has the Son has life; he who does not have the Son of God does not have life. These things I have written to you who believe in the name of the Son of God, that you may know that you have eternal life, and that you may continue to believe in the name of the Son of God.
>
> Now this is the confidence that we have in Him, that if we ask anything according to His will, He hears us. (1 John 5:12–14)

It should not be surprising if people believe easily in a God who makes no demands, but this is not the God of the Bible. Satan has cleverly misled people by whispering that they can believe in Jesus Christ without being changed, but this is the devil's lie. The Bible teaches that belief in Him changes the person. "If anyone loves the world," the Bible says, "the love of the Father is not in him. For all that is in the world—the lust of the flesh, the lust of the eyes, and the pride of life—is not of the Father but is of the world" (1 John 2:15–16).

To those who say you can have Christ without giving anything up, Satan is deceiving you. Do you become part of your country's military force by just saying you are? No, you join up, knowing that it may cost you your life. Before you ever put on a uniform, you must swear an oath, undergo extreme training, and submit yourself to superiors. The wonderful thing about Christianity is that when God's grace saves, God's Spirit moves in and makes the changes possible. Love for the world is replaced with love for God and the things that please Him. If this is not a burning desire, then a person has reason to question the authenticity of his or her faith.

Martin Luther said, "A religion that gives nothing, costs nothing, and suffers nothing, is worth nothing."[48] We can have faith in Jesus Christ because He sacrificed everything—His life's blood. He suffered the pain of every sin that man could imagine, and He is worthy of all our surrender of self to the Savior. We give it all up . . . and in return we get all of Him. This is what the Bible means to be "clothed with salvation" (2 Chronicles 6:41). This is what it means when it says to be "in Christ" (2 Corinthians 5:17). What richness there is in Him.

That's not to say we should expect Jesus to make us rich . . . or beautiful . . . or give us whatever our hearts desire. Becoming a Christian means God will provide for our needs according to His standard, which is higher than ours. We exchange our wills for His will.

The Bible says that we are "enriched in everything by Him" (1 Corinthians 1:5). He changes our countenance to reflect His heart, which is righteous. He begins a work in us that will transform our selfish desires into what He desires so that we glorify Him. He replaces what is most important to us with Himself, and He becomes the most important thing in our lives. Why? Because He is going to guide our every step.

Jesus is bigger than life, so when He comes into yours, there is no room for anything that does not glorify Him. When Jesus came to earth as a baby there was no room in the inn. And people today still refuse to make room for Him in their hearts.

What about you? Will you make room for Him?

You cannot offer Him a stool in the corner of your heart. When He comes into your life, it is because you have set yourself aside as you stand in His presence. In doing so, He will sit on the throne of your life and teach you His truth, and His Spirit will transform your spirit. He becomes the center of life for the Christian where the mind, heart, soul, and body are focused on the glory of Christ.

Are you willing? He seeks and saves those who are lost in sin (Luke 19:10). They exchange living in sin for living in Christ. Do you hear His voice? If so, that is the Holy Spirit speaking to you.

You may listen to many voices that tell you what it means to be a Christian, but here is what Jesus said:

> He who loves father or mother more than Me is not worthy of Me. And he who loves son or daughter more than Me is not worthy of Me. And he who does not take his cross and follow after Me is not worthy of Me. He who finds his life will lose it, and he who loses his life for My sake will find it. (Matthew 10:37–39)

These are hard words, aren't they? The crowds who followed Jesus thought they were hard as well. But taking up His cross means to identify with the suffering of Jesus and accept his lordship. This is the glory of the cross.

I have often emphasized that becoming a Christian is more than making a decision to live a better life or to attend church more regularly. When we receive Jesus as Lord and Savior, something happens supernaturally. Christ comes to dwell in our hearts and gives us His own supernatural life—eternal life. But it is a mistake to imagine that from then on we are automatically and almost magically victorious over sin and doubt. Not so!

Each day we must have the same trust we experienced when we first came to know Christ. This is made possible by the fact that He becomes the predominant Person in our life and empowers us to think differently, to walk in truth, and to follow an upright path.

The Bible says,

> "Now the just [the righteous] shall live by faith;
> But if anyone draws back,
> My soul has no pleasure in him."

But we are not of those who draw back . . . but of those who believe to the saving of the soul. (Hebrews 10:38–39)

We cannot do this in our own power, nor does the power come before we receive Jesus as Savior. It comes when we receive Him as the Lord and Master of our lives, and we cannot live this kind of life apart from Him. This is what it means to be a Christian. And this is the secret of living the Christian life—everyday faith, trusting Him every moment. Each day we renew our faith in God's assurance that He will give us the faith to follow Him.

COUNT THE COST

I am afraid that many Christians, in their zeal to share their faith in Christ, have made the Gospel message of making disciples for Him too simple. Just to say "believe in Christ" can produce a false assurance of the hope of Heaven. Jesus spoke often about the gift of eternal life. To make it clear, He said, "Count the cost."

What does that mean? When Jesus traveled the countryside, great crowds sought Him. They were called *disciples* because they followed Him and longed to hear Him preach. But He knew many of them desired to see His great miracles more than hear His words, so He told them: "Which of you, intending to build a tower, does not sit down first and count the cost? . . . So likewise, whoever of you does not forsake all that he has cannot be My disciple" (Luke 14:28, 33).

Jesus emphasized this more personally when He told a crowd that had gathered, "For I have come down from heaven, not to do My own will, but the will of Him who sent Me" (John 6:38). He went on to tell them that He would die and be raised to life and that those who follow Him must be willing to identify with Him in death and in life. Just as Jesus did the will of His Father, so too must Christians do His will.

> Many of His disciples, when they heard this, said, "This is a hard saying; who can understand it?"
>
> When Jesus knew in Himself that His disciples complained about this, He said to them, "Does this offend you? What then if you should see the Son of Man ascend where He was before? It is the Spirit who gives life; the flesh profits nothing. The words that I speak to you are spirit, and they are life. But there are some of you who do not believe." (John 6:60–64)

Then the Bible makes a startling statement: "From that time many of His disciples went back and walked with Him no more" (v. 66).

These followers loved the excitement of Jesus' miracles. They were drawn to His compassion and mercy extended to the poor and hurting. They were captivated with His promise of eternal life. But they were repelled by His insistence that they must count the cost and identify with Him in death. His words revealed the truth—they were disciples in name only—and they walked away from the truth because their faith was insincere. This is illustrated in the sad account of a successful young man—often called the rich young ruler—who sought Jesus, wanting eternal life, salvation. In fact, the Bible says that he actually "came running" and "knelt before Him" (Mark 10:17), urgently seeking truth. Every preacher, every pastor, every evangelist, and every true disciple of Christ longs to meet such a seeker and answer the question he poses.

Every time I read this story in Matthew, Mark, or Luke, I am moved with compassion because of how Jesus dealt with him—in love but also in truth. The young man respectfully knelt at the feet of Jesus and said, "Good Teacher, what good thing shall I do that I may have eternal life?" (Matthew 19:16).

And Jesus answered the young man very directly. "Why do you call Me good? No one is good but One, that is, God. But if you want to enter into life, keep the commandments" (v. 17).

The young man gave an interesting response by asking *which* commandments he must keep. That answer alone indicates that there were some he knew he hadn't kept; otherwise, he would have answered, "I have kept all the commandments." But it is impossible for anyone to answer that way because the Bible tells us that no one is good apart from God.

Jesus listed some of the commandments. The young man assured Jesus that he had kept all of those. Then he asked, "What do I still lack?" (Matthew 19:20).

The Bible says,

Then Jesus, looking at him, loved him, and said to him, "One thing you lack: Go your way, sell whatever you have and give to the poor, and you will have treasure in heaven; and come, take up the cross, and follow Me."

But he was sad at this word, and went away sorrowful, for he had great possessions. (Mark 10:21–22)

This is one of the most misunderstood passages in the New Testament. Many think that Jesus was giving a requirement for salvation. But there is no work we can do to earn salvation. Jesus paid our ransom with His blood. Rather, Jesus knew the young man's heart. Scripture gives us this astonishing picture of the love Christ has, even for those who reject His truth, for we see here that He gazed at the young man and loved him.

The eyes of the Savior looked into this heart and saw that while he desired eternal life, having it wasn't the burning passion of his life. And while he boasted that he had kept the commandments, he was actually in violation of the very first commandment, "You shall have no other gods before me" (Exodus 20:3). In essence, Jesus was telling him to count the cost. This rich man was knocked off his self-proclaimed pedestal of goodness. He thought he was willing to do whatever necessary to receive this gift, but when he learned the truth about himself, he rejected the truth for self-centeredness.

He had come to the right Source. He asked Jesus to design something "good" for him to do, but he didn't like the solution. When Jesus exposed the young man's own lack of truthfulness, it was evident that he didn't want to be saved from what kept him from eternal life. His riches were too precious to him.

He convinced himself that he was good, but his encounter with Jesus showed him otherwise. His designer world crumbled when he could not obtain salvation because of his refusal to give up his almost-perfect world. The very thing he already had—great wealth—was what kept him from accepting the very thing he requested—the treasure of Heaven, eternal life. The Bible says, "[Jesus] is the true God and eternal life" (1 John 5:20).

This would-be believer stood to his feet and walked away in sorrow. Why? When he counted the cost of his vast fortune, he was not willing to give up the world that suited him. He didn't want to be saved out of what mastered him if it meant making room for Christ to be the Master of his life.

Giving up something to follow Christ is not earning salvation; it is giving up what keeps you from salvation. When we hold on to something that is dearer to us than receiving the greater gift of salvation in Christ, we lose.

Simon Greenleaf, chief legal figure in the early days of Harvard Law School, said, "The object of man's worship, whatever it be, will naturally be his standard of perfection. He clothes it with every attribute, belonging, in his view, to a perfect character; and this character he himself endeavors to attain."[49]

The story of the rich young ruler cuts to the heart of what it means to belong to the world—or to the world you are trying to personally design. It also cuts to the heart of what it means to be a Christian.

What's the difference? you may ask. Belonging to the world means that you do whatever it takes to be part of it, to relate to it at every level—to be joined to its philosophy and purpose, believing that it will bring happiness. That is the devil's lie.

To be a Christian means to surrender yourself to the lordship of Jesus Christ, to give up whatever stands between you and the Lord. This is God's truth.

You must be willing to be changed. Oh, don't try to clean up your life before coming to Christ. It cannot be done in your own power. But you must *desire* to be changed—redesigned. When Christ comes into a life, He gives the power to turn from sinful ways and walk a different path—His path of right living—because He changes our desires. But if we continue to feed our desires and serve our imaginations, there is reason to doubt our Christianity.

An article in the Furman University alumni magazine entitled "Finding Faith," observed that

> The belief system [of many young people today] . . . consists of four parts. First, there is a God, or higher power. . . . Second, God wants people to be good and nice. . . . Third, the central goal in life is to be happy. . . . Finally . . . God [becomes] involved in . . . lives only when needed. . . . Adolescents seem to think of God as a combination of a divine butler and cosmic therapist.[50]

And why not? They live in a culture where "the individual has become the center of society, and therefore focusing on and developing ourselves as individuals is of utmost importance."[51]

Many people who think about becoming Christians ask, "What's in it for me? How can I benefit?" If the answer is only to keep you from Hell, you haven't considered the cost of living for Christ on earth.

The right question is not, "What's in it for me?" but rather, "Is Christ in me?" That very idea is unsettling for many because it means forfeiting control. It means the Lord Jesus Christ will come into your life and reform, conform, and transform you into an obedient follower. If that is not your desire, you have every reason to question whether or not you have been saved.

Most people are not willing to take their hands off their lives to that extent. But this is Christ's offer. When you acknowledge your sin and ask His forgiveness, He cleanses you from the sin that has entangled you and kept you estranged from Him: immorality, pride, selfishness—it is all sin just the same. The great sacrificial work of the Lord Jesus was accomplished for you. For Him to save you and then leave you to clean up your life would be impossible. So the Lord Jesus moves in and takes up residence in your life. That means things are going to change.

God does not expect you to transform yourself before coming to Him in repentance. He calls you to Himself just as you are. But don't make the mistake of thinking He is going to leave you in your sinful state, for that would negate His work on your behalf.

The Trap

The Bible has a lot to say about belonging. The great prophet Daniel spoke about the search for belonging when he prayed, "O Lord, to us belongs shame . . . because we have sinned against You." But, he adds, "To the Lord our God belong mercy and forgiveness, though we have rebelled against Him. We have not obeyed the voice of the LORD our God, to walk in His laws, which He set before us" (Daniel 9:8–10).

Christians do not belong to this world, and they cannot create their own world. Christians belong to the world where Christ reigns supreme, where He is at the center of everything. For those who sincerely confess their sins to Jesus Christ and sincerely want to follow Him, they will "be longing" for a different kind of world, absent from the trappings of carnality.

What is carnality? Living a life consumed by satisfying fleshly desires, feeding selfishness while serving the body and starving the soul. Carnality is the state of depravity. Even the dictionary defines it as "the opposite of righteousness." Those who desire to become Christians must not long to live in such a state of self-service. Belonging to Jesus Christ will cost you your sinful pleasures. You cannot invite holy God into your life and continue in sin.

It is human nature to desire something cheap and easy. Christ's requirements were so demanding that many people refused to go with Him any further. They would go so far, and then they would turn away. That is why He made such a point of telling the crowds who followed Him, "Count the cost . . . count the cost . . . count the cost."

Jesus is saying to you as well: "If you follow Me, that means I become Lord and Master of your life. That means you become My learner, My disciple. And you must do My work by obeying My commands. You must be willing to take up My cross and follow Me. I died for you on that cross. I was tortured and executed on that cross to win your freedom. That means you must turn your back on sin. You will have to stand strong in My name even when it means being subject to abuse and ridicule."

I can remember visiting with a successful businessman who lost his job and position because he refused to cover for top executives who were padding their expense accounts. He was distraught, but he knew covering for dishonesty would tarnish his testimony for the Lord. He put his confidence in the Lord instead of the power of others and eventually led one of the perpetrators to Christ. He counted the cost—a personal cost—and had the joy of winning a soul to Christ.

That won't be easy. But if you let others see Christ in you, He will strengthen you and give you a boldness you have never known. He doesn't ask us to live the Christian life alone. *I* cannot live the Christian life alone. But Christ can live it through me if I will let Him, and He will do the same for you. The reward of His shed blood was the saving of lost souls.

Who said that becoming a Christian was easy? It certainly was not

Jesus. Going to the cross for us was no easy task for Him—it cost Him His life's blood. Being resurrected was no easy happening—it took a miracle. "Easy believism" is an insult to the ultimate sacrifice Jesus made for us. The reward of His shed blood was the saving of lost souls.

Today people are charmed by the love of God without realizing the curse of God's judgment. Multitudes claim to follow Jesus but curse the changes He demands. The Bible says, "Now by this we know that we know Him, if we keep His commandments. He who says, 'I know Him,' and does not keep His commandments, is a liar, and the truth is not in him" (1 John 2:3–4).

There are two roads of life, the world's path and God's path. Imagine a very wide road filled with people, all walking in the same direction. In the center of that road is a narrow path that goes in the opposite direction—it can be a lonely road—but it's the right road. Jesus plainly pointed out these two roads. One is broad, lacking in faith, convictions, and morals. It is the easy, popular, careless way. It is heavily traveled, but it leads to destruction. The other road is narrow and unpopular. This is why Jesus said, "Enter by the narrow gate. For the gate is wide and the way is easy that leads to destruction, and those who enter by it are many. For the gate is narrow and the way is hard that leads to life, and those who find it are few" (Matthew 7:13–14 ESV).

People who follow the broad path are shallow. The path they choose is riddled with compromise. Standing for Christ means that you will walk the narrow way and stand for righteousness, honesty, goodness, morality, and justice. This is not easy in our world today.

Perhaps you are at a crossroads. You find yourself gazing into the faces of those living for popularity and self-pleasure. That road leads to Hell. You are right to look at the narrow path and consider the journey. It can bring persecution because of faith in Christ, but He will walk with you because this is the road that leads to Heaven.

The work that Jesus Christ does is transforming. He does not do a superficial work. When doctors prescribe medication, its purpose is to begin healing the diseased organs and tissue deep inside of us. When

Christ grants salvation, He begins a lifetime work deep within the heart. Change begins inwardly and comes to the surface. The Bible says, "He who has begun a good work in you will complete it until the day of Jesus Christ" (Philippians 1:6).

Just as the characters on the television program *Belonging* struggle with their changing environment, those who are truly saved by Jesus Christ cannot stay the same once they have met Him at the foot of the cross, and carrying that cross will bring struggles and testing. But we are told, "Count it all joy when you fall into various trials, knowing that the testing of your faith produces patience. But let patience have its perfect work, that you may be . . . complete, lacking nothing" (James 1:2–4).

The rich young ruler asked what he was lacking, but when he was given the remedy, he was unwilling to apply it. The Bible says, "Salvation belongs to the LORD" (Psalm 3:8). God has opened the door of faith (Acts 14:27). Those truly seeking salvation will run to Jesus, kneel before Him, examine their hearts in His presence, confess their sin, and renounce whatever is standing between them and the Savior. They will surrender it all to Christ, who will forgive and grant the faith to believe in His power to move into their hearts and transform their lives. HE WILL MAKE THEM FIT FOR ETERNAL LIFE WITH HIM IN THAT WONDERFUL SOMEPLACE CALLED HEAVEN.

Those who belong to Christ Jesus have crucified
the flesh with its passions and desires.
(GALATIANS 5:24 NIV)

CHAPTER SEVEN

NO HOPE OF HAPPY HOUR IN HELL

How shall we escape if we neglect so great a salvation,
which at the first began to be spoken by the Lord.

—HEBREWS 2:3

WHAT DO PEOPLE THINK ABOUT HELL? It may surprise you to know that the subject is not far from peoples' minds, hearts, and lips. Some spoof it, others curse it, many debate it, and some say they want to go there; but the truth is that from the beginning of time, a great many people have lived in dreadful fear of this place called Hell.

Some years ago the subject of Hell had become part of the ash heap of ancient history to many. But largely due to scientific probes, human curiosity, and, to a degree, cultish speculation about the "underworld," there has been a resurging interest in this place of doom. In fact, there's more talk about Hell from the world than there is from the church pulpit.

Hell, for many, is no more than a swear word, and to them sin is also an accepted way of life. People look to science, education, and social and moral programs as possible solutions to the growing chaos of an insane world. If people can ignore what the Bible says about sin, they feel they can discount what it says about the reality of Hell. Whoever chooses to deny that there is a Hell must then face the question: "If I don't go to Heaven when I die, what is the alternative?" We have been so descriptive of the glories of Heaven that we have failed to mention the horrors of its alternative. Pop culture has driven the attitude of tolerance, and one of the many results has been to discard the biblical description of hellfire and brimstone. But some factions are actually taking a closer look at what others want to believe is a myth.

HELL'S IMAGE

The *Boston Globe* reported that Hell experts—"scholars who spend this life studying the next one"—describe Hell as a "place, often beneath the earth, where sinners are punished, where the devil reigns and God is absent."[1] The article contrasts the waning of hellfire-and-brimstone preaching to the vast secular works on the subjects of Heaven and Hell.

The debate about Hell blazes in every sector of life—from science to social media, from nonfiction to novels, from education to entertainment, from international news to the Internet, from ancient history to the coming of the Apocalypse, from the garden of Eden to the twenty-first century.

A publisher's blurb for *The History of Hell*, written from a secular perspective, states: "From the beginning of recorded history people all over the world have believed in an afterlife with two principle destinations, and Hell has inspired more interest than Heaven."[2]

A book from Cornell University Press, *The Formation of Hell*, is hailed for being "highly relevant to a lively debate . . . currently being waged among theologians and philosophers. Traditional views of hell are again receiving serious attention."[3]

The author of a suspense novel, *The Descent*, was asked why he chose to write about Hell. He stated,

> If you're going to descend, really descend. . . . Go to the real heart of darkness, into the underworld . . . [transcend] our remembered nature. Some of the oldest adventure stories . . . have painted a picture of what hell might look like. . . . I serve it up in twenty-first-century style. . . .
>
> Forget the sadist with a pitch fork—that's a cartoon. I tried to envision [Satan] as a real being . . . a philosopher-king, or a guerrilla-leader . . . or a wanderer . . . or a dark prince. . . .
>
> I follow a think tank of elderly scholars as they try to profile the Great Deceiver.[4]

Another twenty-first-century book, *When All Hell Breaks Loose*, offers readers "a new-found confidence regarding survival before crises occur."[5] But the truth about eternal survival is found in the most enduring Book, the Bible. "I give them eternal life, and they shall never perish" (John 10:28).

Heaven and Hell are realities just as life and death are realities, and Jesus used the strongest language to describe the repulsiveness of Hell. While people disapprove of Jesus' description of Hell, they find themselves at a loss to describe this ominous place any differently.

A major newspaper carried the headline "Earth's Center Hotter than Sun's Surface."[6] *Discover* magazine quoted a geologist who said, "It's quite clear that the core [of the earth] is a more hostile environment than the surface of the sun."[7] The article is fascinating because all the experts interviewed agreed that it is not possible to know just how hostile the earth's core really is unless, as the author said, "we actually trekked down to Earth's center."[8] Even though science has tried to disprove the Bible, it has substantiated that at the center of the earth lies a molten, volcanic domain. This very well could be the place that Jesus called the "lake of fire" in Revelation 19 and 20.

The *Atlas Obscura* reports a fire hole in the Karakum desert of Turkmenistan (Russia) called the Gates of Hell.[9] It seems the natural inclination of man is to equate unquenchable fire with Hell, just as Jesus warned: "The fire is not quenched" (Mark 9:44).

Perhaps the most famous depiction of Hell from the literary world is Dante's *Inferno*, part of his classic allegoric poem *The Divine Comedy*. The fourteenth-century Italian poet wrote about a journey to Hell, where he was welcomed by a sign, "All hope abandon, ye who enter in!" a place occupied by all those who are unrepentant of sin.[10]

The *Inferno* was inspired by an earlier work from Titus Lucretius Carus, born about a century before Jesus Christ. The *New Yorker* magazine ran a several-page article concerning Hell from the perspective of Lucretius, as expressed in his famous poem "On the Nature of Things." It is said that the core of his poem is "a profound, therapeutic meditation on the fear of death."[11] The author stated, "To people . . . gripped by a terror of Hell, and obsessed with escaping the . . . fires of the afterlife, Lucretius offered a vision of divine indifference. There was no afterlife, no system of rewards and punishments meted out from on high. Gods, by virtue of being gods, could not possibly be concerned with the doings of human beings"[12]—therefore, no Hell.

After Lucretius's ideas were rediscovered in the fifteenth century, his work began to catch on in the forms of atomism and atheism,[13] a total rejection that a supreme being is the architect of human life. Others tried to build on the emptiness by developing ideas like those expressed in *Utopia*, a notorious work by Thomas More in which the inhabitants of his imaginary land find ultimate happiness in the pursuit of pleasure. "His use of [Lucretius's] philosophy for the population of this alien island showed that the ideas recovered by the humanists seemed . . . utterly weird."[14] Why? Because his theory had no substantive source. These philosophers put their faith in nature, which led them to worship nature.

The Bible says this: "When you did not know God, you served those which by nature are not gods" (Galatians 4:8). Mankind's nature is to worship everything but God.

Would you align your life to just another man's idea? Many, unfortunately, do. Some say that having faith in a higher being is preposterous but will give themselves up to the idea of utopia.

But utopia still has not put to rest the curiosity of Hell. French sculptor Auguste Rodin was commissioned in 1880 to create a multifaceted piece called *The Gates of Hell.* The finished work included the famous *The Thinker,* which some questioned whether it was a depiction of the first man, Adam, "contemplating the destruction brought upon mankind for his sin."[15]

Most think that "good people" who mind their own business should have some eternal rewards. These people say, "Surely a loving God would not punish good people." They are right in that God does not want them to go to Hell. "God our Savior . . . desires all men to be saved" (1 Timothy 2:3–4).

The problem is not that Hell exists, for it must, since God is holy. Rather we must distinguish between the biblical meanings of good and evil because the problem is that men don't want to understand that sin is offensive in the eyes of a supremely holy God. Sin is not rated by a scale. Hell is eternal separation from God and can be pardoned only by a truly supreme sacrifice, accomplished by the substitutionary death of the Son of God on the cross. The afterlife is determined in the land of the living by how people respond to Jesus' sacrifice of Himself to rescue lost souls, "snatching them from the fire" (Jude 23 NIV).

When the science-fiction author Isaac Asimov was interviewed on the subject of Heaven and Hell, he stated, "I don't believe in hell or the afterlife."[16] Elsewhere he added to that statement: "I don't believe . . . so I don't have to spend my whole life fearing hell, or fearing heaven even more. For whatever the tortures of hell, I think the boredom of heaven would be even worse."[17]

To fear Hell seems obvious, but to fear Heaven even more? Why would that be? Because humans know instinctively that to look into the face of holy God produces one certainty: the truth of man's sin and his rejection of Almighty God. "No flesh will be justified in [God's] sight, for by the law is the knowledge of sin" (Romans 3:20).

WHO SAYS THERE'S HAPPY HOUR IN HELL?

It has been said that the devil's greatest work is to convince people Hell doesn't exist. Some fool themselves by saying, "If there is a Hell, it will be a devil of a party." Others say, "No devil, no sin; no sin, no guilt; no guilt, no need to repent; no repentance, no need for God."

But the Bible says the Gospel "is veiled to those who are perishing, whose minds the god of this age has blinded, who do not believe" (2 Corinthians 4:3–4). "I fear," Paul wrote, "lest somehow, as the serpent deceived Eve by his craftiness, so your minds may be corrupted from the simplicity that is in Christ" (2 Corinthians 11:3).

French biologist and philosopher Jean Rostand said, "I should have no use for a paradise in which I should be deprived of the right to prefer hell."[18] This, indeed, is a breathtaking admission, but the truth is that people's confession of preferring Hell is simply a cover-up for their unwillingness to confess that Jesus Christ is Lord and humble themselves before Him.

Singer/songwriter John Lennon is famous for his ballad "Imagine," which invites people to visualize an existence where there is no Heaven, no Hell, no religion, and everybody is "living for today."[19] But saying there is no Hell doesn't make it so. This is precisely what the Bible is talking about when it describes people who "became vain in their imaginations, and their foolish heart was darkened" (Romans 1:21 KJV).

Satan creates religion without a Redeemer. He builds church without Christ. He calls for worship without the Word of God. The Bible says that Satan's work is to deceive the world (Revelation 12:9), and his deception that Hell is where the party will be is a clever trick. He is called "an angel of light" (2 Corinthians 11:14) because he disguises evil in whatever attracts the senses. Many think Hell will be no more than the hottest "happy hour" and more fun than Heaven.

The idea that there will be a great fellowship of sinners in Hell has no biblical basis whatsoever. Hell, in Scripture, is described as solitary confinement, where a sinner's companion will not be his imagination, but his memory (Luke 16:25).

An emerging trend in places like Bangkok, Thailand, is the underworld amusement park that exalts the dark side of the afterlife. The entrance to Wang Saen Suk Hell Gardens says, "Welcome to Hell." Visitors are "entertained" in a "land of tortured, wretched souls suffering an eternal life of misery . . . send[ing] out a clear message: judgment day will come."[20]

Popularizing Hell in today's culture has turned it into a fashionable destination. This is the depravity of the human soul, terrorizing self with evil and growing accustomed to hellish entertainment branded by the world's system and lifestyle as fun.

Some may say these are samples of the fringe of society, but sadly, this culture has become mainstream. South African journalists have covered this phenomenon not only from Cape Town but around the world. "Whole communities . . . profit from, an extensive, multi-million rand [the main unit of South African currency] underworld economy. And there's a good chance you are part of it," the article states, adding that "The underworld economy endures. . . . It is no longer a fringe activity."[21]

In an effort to diminish fear of eternal damnation, mankind has concocted an antidote: become so familiar with Hell that it no longer provokes anxiety—or joke about Hell in hopes the laughter will snuff out the searing fire that brings oppression. Perhaps this was the thinking behind the musical *Hell Ain't a Bad Place to Be*, which premiered in Australia in 2011.[22] Recording artist Billy Joel sings that sinners "are much more fun" than saints.[23] But the Bible disagrees. The truth is that in Heaven God will wipe all tears away (Revelation 21:4), but Hell will be a place of weeping (Matthew 8:12)—a very bad place to be.

Some comedians spoof Hell without a flinch. Talk-show host Conan O'Brien has repeatedly entertained his audience with this lyric: "I can't

be saved, it's too late for me. I'm going to H-E Double L when I D-I-E."[24]
Comedian Kathy Griffin, whose website promotes her cable television
specials entitled "Kathy Griffin: Straight to Hell,"[25] says, "I know I'm
going straight to Hell. I have my handbasket all decorated."[26]

This type of humor is cloaked in despair and utter darkness, coming
from the lips of people who do not realize that their laughing will turn
to wailing. Those who trivialize the boding evil of Hell do not care for
peoples' souls. They court the devil who bids them to Hell while they
ignore the voice of God that is still saying to all people, "Come to Me."

Jesus warned people about Hell out of the depths of His love and
compassion, to prevent people *from ever knowing* this gruesome reality.
This is what the Bible says:

> Do you despise the riches of [God's] goodness, forbearance, and
> longsuffering, not knowing that the goodness of God leads you to
> repentance? But in accordance with your hardness and your impeni-
> tent heart you are treasuring up for yourself wrath in the day of wrath
> and revelation of the righteous judgment of God . . . to those who are
> self-seeking and do not obey the truth, but obey unrighteousness—
> indignation and wrath, tribulation and anguish, on every soul of man
> who does evil. (Romans 2:4–9)

The world would have us think that Hell is a night-thriller, but Hell is a
hungry reaper.

Nobel Prize winner George Bernard Shaw, speaking of Hell, said,

> Written over the gate here are the words "Leave every hope behind, ye
> who enter." Only think what a relief that is! For what is hope? A form
> of moral responsibility. Here there is no hope, and consequently no
> duty, no work, nothing to be gained by praying, nothing to be lost by
> doing what you like. Hell, in short, is a place where you have nothing
> to do but amuse yourself.[27]

The truth is that free time in Hell will be consumed with remembering. Wallowing in memories of rejecting God will not be amusing.

A story is told of two fathers who took their teenage sons camping. They built a roaring fire and warned the boys to stay far from it, asking them to gather more wood. The boys carelessly ignored the instruction and laughed behind their fathers' backs. As the two dads erected the tents, the boys wrestled with one another and recklessly fell into the fire pit, where the flames caught their hair and clothing. For the rest of their lives, they lived with the scars of the fateful night they scorned their fathers' loving command. Memories of that incident didn't bring laughter and good times; there was horrific regret and torment of mind and body.

THE ROAD TO HELL

Human nature is inclined to resist authority, and this is why people are offended when they hear about the truth of Hell. Professor Alan Cairns made the thought-provoking statement, "How many millions there are who don't want to go to Hell, but they don't want to get off the road to Hell."[28] We are a rebellious people prone to crave what satisfies our sensual and selfish appetites without thought of consequences.

The Bible describes our nature like this:

> "How I have hated instruction,
> And my heart despised correction!" . . .
> For the ways of man are before the eyes of the Lord,
> And He ponders all his paths. . . .
> He is caught in the cords of his sin.
> He shall die for lack of instruction,
> And in the greatness of his folly he shall go astray.
> (Proverbs 5:12, 21–23)

Many are repulsed by the command to live obedient and holy lives. Job spoke of those who lived for pleasure and selfish desires, who said to God,

> "Depart from us,
> For we do not desire the knowledge of Your ways.
> Who is the Almighty, that we should serve Him?"
>
> (JOB 21:14–15)

While we feed on the very things that cause us harm, our minds lead us astray. "To those who are defiled and unbelieving nothing is pure; but even their mind and conscience are defiled" (Titus 1:15).

Have you ever asked yourself, *What is uplifting about entertainment that glorifies the gore of Hell?* So many are being enticed by the mysteries of films such as *Drag Me to Hell* (2009), *The Gates of Hell* (2008), and *The City of the Living Dead* (1980—also called *The Gates of Hell*). Movie posters and online advertisements promote these movies with dreadful warnings: "Evil breeds beyond . . . *The Gates of Hell*."[29]

Here is the truth: Satan desires to drag the world along the road that leads to Hell, his designated place of darkness. He takes advantage of each person's freedom to choose. You see, it is not God who condemns people to Hell. The people themselves do that when they defiantly reject God. The real city of the living dead is indeed the place of dwelling doom. The risk is ours to take, but choosing Satan's lie over God's love brings unending horror more grim than the worst nightmare. Those who choose to go there will never wake up with hope, for a person who is condemned to Hell will never know rest. The suffering separation from God will never end.

What road are you traveling?

THE REALM OF BATTLE

There is a mighty battle for people's souls taking place in the heavenly realms between the God of Heaven and Satan's domain. How else can we explain humanity's eagerness to listen to vulgarity and run after immorality if the spirit of evil is not empowered by Satan?

The Bible says, "For we do not wrestle against flesh and blood, but against . . . powers, against the rulers of the darkness of this age, against spiritual hosts of wickedness" (Ephesians 6:12). If you hear a voice that tells you Hell is not for real, believe God's truth—not Satan's lie.

You may rightly ask, "What is the difference in watching a film about Hell or reading about Hell in the Bible?" There is a great chasm of difference. When you seek entertainment that puts the spotlight on Hell and its forces, you are inviting a satanic presence into your thought life. When you read Scripture about Hell, you are exposing your mind to the truth of what God has done to keep you from this imposing force. Don't reap the results of Hell's abomination; heed the warning that comes from God's appraisal of this inconsolable place, for the Bible says that He will "punish the world for its evil" (Isaiah 13:11).

Many may close their eyes to the consequence of Hell and take sinful delight in what Satan offers. Many, who claim they do not believe in God, believe enough to ridicule Him for Hell's existence. This clearly reveals that down deep in their souls they know God is who He says He is. Otherwise they would not have such vehement hatred of the truth—that He knows the motives of the heart.

The reality of Hell is that God created it for Satan and his demons. "The everlasting fire [is] prepared for the devil and his angels" (Matthew 25:41). God does not desire anyone to follow Satan to this daunting place. That's why Scripture commands us to "resist the devil and he will flee" (James 4:7). But this is only possible for those who belong to the Lord. He is the One who strengthens us.

Satan is constantly after us while we still have the freedom to choose. He is "the prince of the power of the air, the spirit who now works in the sons of disobedience, among whom also we all once conducted ourselves in the lusts of our flesh, fulfilling the desires of the flesh and of the mind" (Ephesians 2:2–3). We must beware of opening our minds to him.

Satan is well acquainted with the world of television and uses it powerfully to deceive. Twentieth Century Fox produced an animated series for kids about a family of demons who come up to live on earth and discover that "humans can be more evil than any demon ever could." The show was called *Neighbors from Hell*.[30]

The Bible does not talk about a family from Hell, but it does describe the family that will be in Hell. Jesus said,

> If God were your Father, you would love Me, for I proceeded forth and came from God. . . . Why do you not understand My speech? Because you are not able to listen to My word. You are of your father the devil, and the desires of your father you want to do. He was a murderer from the beginning, and does not stand in the truth, because there is no truth in him. When he speaks a lie, he speaks from his own resources, for he is a liar and the father of it. But because I tell the truth, you do not believe Me. . . . He who is of God hears God's words; therefore you do not hear, because you are not of God. (John 8:42–47)

Many people call God the Father of the human race, but the Bible teaches that God is the Creator. Satan is the father of those who reject Christ and run after the world's system. Those who have accepted Christ and obediently follow Him as Lord belong to the Father in Heaven. Who do you belong to?

The Bible tells us, "Humble yourselves under the mighty hand of God. . . . Be sober, be vigilant; because your adversary the devil walks about like a roaring lion, seeking whom he may devour" (1 Peter 5:6, 8). You may ask, "Just how does he do that?" Through whatever means he can. The devil's workshop is in the airwaves, in the environment, in the depths of the earth, and in the hearts of human beings. Even cyberspace is permeated with hellbent propaganda.

While the Internet can be a resource for good, it is also a powerful billboard that draws victims to sites such as Hell.com, with a logo of a black box with an arrow pointing downward; proclaimed as a "mysterious place for Net-artists to hang out"[31] and "where [the founder] simply messed with visitors' heads."[32] You may be surprised that the Bible warns about entering such places:

> Do not enter the path of the wicked. . . .
> Avoid it, do not travel on it.
>
> (PROVERBS 4:14–15)

> Woe to those who call evil good, and good evil;
> Who put darkness for light, and light for darkness.
>
> (ISAIAH 5:20)

Society has become obsessed with leisure, and both kids and adults are enchanted with the latest craze in video games. Don't think for a minute that Satan has overlooked this pastime. One site describes Hell, as used in video games, as "the home of evil incarnate," and "the use of Hell tends to be closely tied to a game's use of demons and holy objects or crusades."[33] In a conversation with one mother, she stated that this was a creative way to teach her kids about Hell without having to take it too seriously. The Bible warns about such activity: "And even as they did not like to retain God in their knowledge, God gave them over to a debased mind. . . . they are . . . inventors of evil things" (Romans 1:28–30).

With entertainment technology today, there are few boundaries that prevent diverse entertainment from being viewed or heard by any age and in almost any nation. The Brazilian online magazine *Hell Divine* has released its sixth compilation of heavy-metal music by Brazilian and Portuguese bands. Titled *Upcoming Hell—Volume VI*, it includes music from bands such as Hell Arise, Sacredeath, The Black Coffins, and Warfire.[34]

Hell is anything but divine; it is a place of torment (Luke 16:19–26). Hell is not upcoming; it is outer darkness (Matthew 8:12). Hell is a place not of sacred death but of perpetual unrest (Revelation 14:11). Hell will not arise; it will be fully realized in the depths of unrepentant souls (Matthew 25:46).

PREOCCUPIED WITH HELL

Many genres of music are also preoccupied with the subject of Hell. The heavy-metal group Metallica sings of selling a soul to the "Angel from below."[35] Australian hard-rock band AC/DC named an album *Highway to Hell*, and its title song announces that the singer is headed down that very road.[36] The band Venom's song "Satanachist" includes the lyric, "I preach the ways of Satan."[37]

There seems to be a flaunting attitude in today's culture about the idea of going to Hell, but in Scripture there is not one example of anyone desiring to go there. In fact, Jesus told the story of a man agonizing in Hell who "cried and said . . . 'Have mercy on me . . . cool my tongue; for I am tormented in this flame'" (Luke 16:23–24).

This man's senses and personality were fully engaged. He had his sight, he had his hearing, he had his speech, he had his taste, he had feeling, and he had his memory. What he did *not* have was hope. He begged for someone to warn his five living brothers of the torment of Hell, saying, "If one goes to them from the dead, they will repent" (v. 30). But the truth is that One did come back from the dead—the Lord Jesus Christ—and mankind still rejected Him. While rejection of Hell does not mean acceptance of Christ, rejection of Christ does mean certainty of Hell.

A band named Heaven & Hell recorded an album in Wales entitled *The Devil You Know*. The album artwork was adapted from a painting entitled *Satan* and featured the numbers 25 and 41. One of the band members explained that the numbers were taken from Matthew 25:41: "Then He will also say to those on the left hand, 'Depart from Me, you cursed, into the everlasting fire prepared for the devil and his angels.'"[38]

Lifting a Scripture verse from its context often causes confusion and lack of understanding. Indeed, a verse like this on its own can sound harsh and unloving. But, you see, Jesus spoke about judgment out of love. Let's put the rest of the story in its proper setting as we consider Matthew 25:41.

Jesus was speaking to large crowds as He sat on the Mount of Olives, overlooking the city of Jerusalem. He was teaching the people about

His coming kingdom, explaining the truth about righteousness and judgment.

Let's not miss the warmth of His beckoning call just a few verses earlier. This is the heart of the Savior who is seeking the lost. "Then the King will say to those on His right hand, 'Come, you blessed of My Father, inherit the kingdom prepared for you from the foundation of the world" (Matthew 25:34). Jesus is still extending this invitation today. "Come to Me, all you who you labor and are heavy laden, and I will give you rest" (Matthew 11:28).

Jesus was telling the crowd that from the beginning of time He has made a way of escape. Man can choose Matthew 25:34, but rejecting Christ will put him right in the midst of Matthew 25:41.

> "For they proceed from evil to evil,
> And they do not know Me. . . .
> Your dwelling place is in the midst of deceit;
> Through deceit they refuse to know Me," says the LORD.
>
> (JEREMIAH 9:3, 6)

Do you stand today with Jesus, or do you stand with Satan? For man there are only two choices. Let me tell you where Jesus stands—at the right hand of God the Father. Just as He hung on the cross with arms stretched out, He stands with open arms to welcome into His kingdom all who will repent, turn from sin, receive His gift of salvation—eternal life—and live for Him in obedience today. If you haven't already settled your destination in the next life, will you today?

HELL IS GOING TO BE A MESS

There are those who believe that people who do good toward their fellow man will escape Hell, but from the billionaire world comes a statement from mogul Ted Turner, named Humanist of the Year in 1990.[39] In response to a statement about Christ dying on the cross, Turner said, "I don't want anybody to die for me. I've had a few drinks and a few girlfriends, and if that's going to put me in hell, then so be it."[40]

When addressing the National Press Club in 1994, Mr. Turner said,

> Heaven's going to be a mighty slender place, and most of the people I know in life aren't going to be there. . . . Heaven is going to be perfect, and I don't really want to be there. . . . Those of us who go to hell, it'll be most of us in this room . . . we'll have a chance to make things better, because hell's supposed to be a mess and heaven's perfect. Who wants to go to a place that's perfect? I mean, boring, boring.[41]

In a 2003 interview, Mr. Turner said, "I was born again seven times, including by Billy Graham."[42] I wish I could sit with Mr. Turner, look him in the eye, and tell him about the redeeming love of God and the righteous judgment of the King of Heaven. The very meaning of the word *righteous* is honorable, respectable, and blameless. Everything Jesus does, even in judgment, is pure and trustworthy. The Bible says,

> [God's] work is perfect;
> For all His ways are justice . . .
> Righteous and upright is He.
>
> (DEUTERONOMY 32:4)

All those in Hell will remember their opportunity for Heaven and will comprehend the perfect justice of their final fate.

I can remember a professor in Bible school saying, "Never preach Hell without tears in your eyes." This is why I cannot read such testimony without it creating in me a heavy heart. God loves the souls of men and women. Jesus died for the souls of mankind. But the Bible says that the Spirit of God will not "strive with man forever" (Genesis 6:3).

I have preached the Gospel for more than seventy years and have always spoken clearly that salvation comes through Christ alone. I cannot save anyone, but I've tried to tell everyone who would listen that Jesus died once for the sins of mankind and that salvation is a one-time transaction between an individual and the Lord Jesus Christ. As for those who continually "get saved" without knowing the transformation of soul, their act of repentance before holy God could be insincere.

Many say if they would be given a miraculous sign from God, they would believe. But the most miraculous of God's work is transforming the sinner's heart into a blood-bought soul that will love Him wholly. God knows the heart of every person and longs to apply His redeeming blood to that person's soul, washing away the darkness of sin and the fear of eternal judgment. But he or she must come to Jesus Christ in brokenness, exchanging sin for salvation.

We talk about the sacrifice that Jesus made for us, but we seldom talk about the sacrifice He expects from us. While salvation is purely the work of Jesus on the cross, our acceptance of it is dependent upon our sincerity. The Bible says,

> The sacrifices of God are a broken spirit,
> A broken and a contrite heart—
> These, O God, You will not despise.
>
> (PSALM 51:17)

I have extended Christ's invitation to people around the world saying, "Come just as you are." But when you come, you must leave your defiance and rebellion behind and come in submission, for in that moment of repentance the Savior of your soul will become the Master of your life. Heaven or Hell is determined for all of us by this absolute truth.

PHILOSOPHY OR TRUTH

Mankind has attempted to explain truth away through philosophy, which is simply human wisdom that lacks authority. This question is asked in the Bible: "So where does this leave the philosophers, the scholars, and the world's brilliant debaters? God has made the wisdom of this world look foolish. . . . God in His wisdom saw to it that the world would never know him through human wisdom" (1 Corinthians 1:20–21 NLT). The ancient scholars, philosophers, and debaters are dead, but we are listening to new scholars, philosophers, and debaters through every communication mode. And still the world is in turmoil to discover peace. Still the human race is frantically searching for truth. Listen to what the Bible says: "Be *still*, and know that I am God" (Psalm 46:10, italics added).

Humanity prefers to put confidence in its own ideas, instead of in the authority of God's Word. The human race rejects God's wisdom because it rejects Him and, therefore, calls His message of truth foolish.

Studies reveal that most people believe in some type of Hell and certainly equate Satan with his place of doom. They may not believe it is a literal place—that is, until you mention the names of mass murderers like Adolf Hitler, Joseph Stalin, Pol Pot, and Osama bin Laden or serial killers like Charles Manson and Jeffrey Dahmer. They don't question their right to pass judgment, saying that these people belong in Hell. Why? Because they judge according to their own definition of evil.

I would ask those same people what judgment they would render to drug pushers responsible for destroying minors, or liars who deceive the elderly, or drunk drivers who snuff out the lives of law-abiding citizens, or pedophiles who rape children of their innocence—or to those who curse the name of the One who gave them life.

These are often the same people who think they have a greater capacity for love than the Savior of the world. They believe they can love more than Christ because they claim they are willing to "live and let live" and that God should do the same.

This is simply arrogance. Only the God of Heaven deserves the right to pass judgment, and He has entrusted this task to the One who suffered the ultimate agony and paid for that right with His own blood. "For the Father judges no one, but has committed all judgment to the Son, that all should honor the Son" (John 5:22–23).

Yet this Man who came to save the world from evil said, "For God did not send His Son into the world to condemn the world, but that the world through Him might be saved. . . . But he who does not believe is condemned already, because he has not believed in the name of the only begotten Son of God" (John 3:17–18).

People condemn others who do evil by their standard but resent holy God who upholds His standard. That is the fundamental problem with humans, thinking they are greater than God. Society glosses over the very One who came to save them from the doom of all evil. Why then do people curse the name of Jesus and think they have the right to call His judgment into question? Why do they think they have the right to condemn others to Hell while they curse the only One who can save them from their own condemnation?

The Bible answers this question: "And this is the condemnation, that the light has come into the world, and men loved darkness rather than light, because their deeds were evil. For everyone practicing evil hates the light and does not come to the light, lest his deeds should be exposed" (vv.19–20).

Just what is evil? The Bible says: "For the wrath of God is revealed from heaven against all ungodliness and unrighteousness of men, who suppress the truth in unrighteousness . . . so that they are without excuse, because, although they knew God, they did not glorify Him as God" (Romans 1:18, 20–21).

With evil intent, mankind has always tried to bring God down to its level. This, in fact, is one of the ways we humans emulate Satan, who desires to be on par with God, though he never will be. Whether mere humans recognize God as Creator, God as all-powerful, God as all-knowing, God as omnipresent doesn't change the fact that He is all these things. If you don't believe this, you are being deceived.

Who are we to denounce His Person? Who are we to defy His power? Who are we to debate His pronouncements? Who are we to decline His pardon?

It is because of His Person that He delivers mankind from sin.

It is through His power that He defeats Satan in the end. It is by His pronouncements that He declares His grace and mercy forever. And how does the world respond? By cursing His name, by accusing His motives, and by thinking created beings higher than the Most High. This sums up the evil works of man.

A WORLD WITHOUT RESTRAINT

Can you imagine what would happen in the world without law enforcement? There would be no restraint, and unbridled wickedness would reign. The world has witnessed what can happen when a country's borders are compromised—those who intend to do harm slip in unnoticed and disguised and then take credit for the evil deeds they do openly. Why are people and nations justified in bringing judgment against those who do harm, but think they can deny God the right to execute holy judgment?

I recall a man who traveled with my son Franklin in the Middle East. They were going to deliver food, clothing, and medicine to refugees in a war-torn area. This young man wanted to do a good work for the people of that country, but there was a problem. He had failed to secure a visa. When he tried to go through customs, the officials said, "Sorry, we do not recognize you as having the credentials to come in." The man had traveled a great distance but was turned away.

You may say, "Well, that's unfair." But you see, he had been told in advance that he would have to go to the consulate to receive the required document, but he thought he could talk his way in. Perhaps he thought his great smile and cheery disposition would carry him through. Perhaps he thought he could explain that he was coming to do great favors for the people. But he had not been justified. He had not met the requirements of that country and was denied entrance.

This is a picture of Heaven. It is revealed through the telescope of God's Word. You must belong to the kingdom of God while on earth to get through the gates of Heaven in the afterlife. The Bible says that the day will come when the Lord will separate mankind into two groups: those who have placed their faith in Him and those who have rejected Him (Matthew 25:31–46).

I would ask, "Why do people who oppose Jesus while they live want to spend eternity with Him in Heaven?" Our level of goodness does not meet the requirement to become citizens in God's country. The requirement is a humble and repentant heart. But as we have seen, human nature makes us resist handing our lives over to another. This is a barrier that keeps many from coming to Christ. They are unwilling to listen to God's Spirit, which calls them to surrender to the One who says, "Come."

We have no power to create, yet we defile the Creator. We have no power over life and death, yet we reject the Giver of life. We cannot possibly know the future, yet we deny Him who holds it in His hand. We are given knowledge, yet we denounce the most valuable knowledge—God's truth. Those who know God "know the spirit of truth and the spirit of error. . . . Love has been [completed] among us in this: that we may have boldness in the day of judgment; because as He is, so are we in this world" (1 John 4:6, 17).

Humans fear the judgment of Hell because they reject the righteous justice of God. Accepting God's truth gives us certainty of His love in the Day of Judgment. The evil work of humanity is suppressing God's truth, which is an abomination in His sight.

MIXING GOOD AND EVIL

Writer Norman Mailer, a two-time Pulitzer Prize winner, stated,

> I'm not interested in absolute moral judgments. . . . Just think of what it means to be a good man or a bad one. What, after all, is the measure of difference? . . . Say I'm 60 percent bad and 40 percent good—for that, must I suffer eternal punishment? . . . Heaven and Hell make no

sense if the majority of humans are a complex mixture of good and evil. That's almost impossible to contemplate.[43]

Contemplate it, my friend, because Jesus said, "The things which are impossible with men are possible with God" (Luke 18:27). Mailer's statement is an example of man thinking he is good when he is full of pride and deception.

The story is told of teenage siblings who asked their father for money to go see a movie with their friends. Knowing the content of the movie was inappropriate, the father told them they couldn't go.

The son and daughter debated their position by telling their father that there were only a few curse words and one minor immoral scene, but the rest of the movie was a wonderful love story with high adventure. The father still refused to let them go.

Sulking, they retreated to their rooms until they were called for supper. When it came time for dessert, their mother set a pan of freshly baked brownies smothered with creamy icing on the table. The father cut large squares for his children and said, "Your mother has made your favorite dessert, but there is one thing you should know before you eat it. I had her mix some manure into the batter."

The teenagers shoved the plates back and tilted away from the table. "How could you?" they moaned.

"Oh, it's just a little bit," the father answered. "Enjoy!"

That lesson, both of them would say later in life, served as a reminder that it takes only a trifle to corrupt. Needless to say, the entire pan of brownies was thrown out.

Sinful man thinks he is good, but he bears the seed of sin. It is God who is good and gracious to forgive the sinner and then plants the seed of holiness within his heart. The Bible says, "No one who is born of God will continue to sin, because God's seed remains in them; they cannot go on sinning" (1 John 3:9 NIV). When God looks at the transformed man, He sees the redemptive work of His Son, who turns men and women from darkness into His marvelous light.

Let me point you to the One who cares for you. You see, escaping Hell is not the main issue. The main issue is the heart of God's message to man, written in blood: "He laid down His life for us" (1 John 3:16).

Even in this jaded, self-centered culture, do we so easily turn away from someone who makes a sacrifice for us? No, most will be indebted and show a spirit of gratitude and service toward the person who made the sacrifice.

When men and women believe they are good enough and powerful enough to control their own destinies, they prove what the Bible says about "having a form of godliness but denying its power" (2 Timothy 3:5). People may be offended by thoughts of Hell, but God is offended by our unbelief in Him. We think we can hide behind masks, thinking we are good, thinking we can laugh off the reality of Hell, but the Bible says that those who offend God will be "cast . . . into the furnace of fire. There will be wailing and gnashing of teeth" (Matthew 13:42).

But this does not have to be your destiny. Listen to what one man wrote after he came out of darkness into the light, even one who had rejected God's Son. Later he looked back in gratitude: "For we ourselves were also once foolish, disobedient, deceived, serving various lusts and pleasures. . . . But when the kindness and the love of God our Savior toward man appeared . . . He saved us . . . to the hope of eternal life" (Titus 3:3–7).

This murderer, named Saul, sought and persecuted those who were following Jesus—until one day, along a highway, he heard God's plea to come to Him (Acts 9). Saul's soul was reformed from sinner to saint. Saul's will was conformed from his to God's. And Saul the man was transformed to Paul the apostle, who gave this profound testimony: "This is a faithful saying and worthy of all acceptance, that Christ Jesus came into the world to save sinners, of whom I am chief" (1 Timothy 1:15).

Don't think you're hopeless. Don't hide behind scoffing, mocking, false humility, and laughter that the world applauds. Jesus said to such people, "You are those who justify yourselves before men, but God knows your hearts. For what is highly esteemed among men is an abomination in the sight of God" (Luke 16:15).

Behind the world's curtain is Satan, pushing people into his vile and wicked world, using them as his mouthpiece to taunt the name of the One who still is saying to a lost world, "Come." Flee the lures of Satan and the judgment of a Christless eternity and come into the care of Christ's everlasting forgiveness, abundant grace, and merciful love.

How do I know He cares for you? Because He says, "Come." How do I know He loves you? Because "while we were still sinners, Christ died for us. Much more then . . . we shall be saved from wrath through Him" (Romans 5:8–9).

Nothing could possibly demonstrate God's love for us more than the provision He has made through forgiving sin. HOPE IN THE LORD IS NOT A WISH BUT AN ABSOLUTE ASSURANCE THAT MAN CAN BE SNATCHED FROM THE FIRE OF DESTRUCTION AND BE SAVED INTO NEW LIFE—CHANGED BY THE MERCY OF JESUS CHRIST AND DECLARED RIGHTEOUS BEFORE HIS THRONE OF GRACE.

For we were saved in this hope . . . we eagerly
wait for it with perseverance.

(ROMANS 8:24–25)

CHAPTER EIGHT

HE IS COMING BACK

For God did not appoint us to wrath, but to obtain salvation
through our Lord Jesus Christ, who died for us, that . . . we
should live together with Him. Therefore comfort each other.

—1 THESSALONIANS 5:9–11

DO YOU THINK HE'S COMING BACK? People flocked to the most highly anticipated Hollywood movie release in the summer of 2012 for the answer.

Who were they talking about? The legendary comic-strip superhero of the 1940s, a caped crusader who triumphs over archvillains. Batman has been idolized in print, on television, and more recently in theaters.

As a boy, I loved comic books and read every one I could get my hands on more than once. The stories I read taught the lesson that evil deeds will be trampled and victory will reign. What was once a form of comic entertainment for children has become cosmic adventure for adults, who find delight in a new pop-culture phenomenon—the emergence of recreational evil. Many see it as frivolous until its reality fills hearts with trepidation.

On July 20, 2012, fans filled movie theaters for the premier of Warner

Brothers' production *The Dark Knight Rises*, in which citizens of the fictitious Gotham City wonder if Batman will come back to save their cosmopolitan way of life from nuclear annihilation.

While the plot is fictional, it profiles humanity's great search to understand good and evil. But an astonishing story emerged when the evil characters—not the hero—seemed to capture the admiration of fans. Many arrived in costumes to mimic the villains.

The Telegraph in London wrote that the movie was a "superhero film without a superhero"[1] because the would-be superstar faltered in many ways and illustrious criminals had a greater allure to wild imaginations. One reviewer noted that Bane, the primary villain, "wears a ventilator mask [and] fills [the] morgue with innocents"[2] and another claimed the Tom Hardy character "was able to execute emotion and intimidate the audience using just his eyes and forehead."[3] The film's director, Christopher Nolan, added in an interview that the character is "very complex and very interesting and . . . people will be very entertained by him."[4] *Newsweek* simply reported that "Audiences will be blown away."[5]

So electrifying was the marketing campaign that people around the world stood in lines at 6:30 in the morning to buy advance tickets while others avoided queues by going online to purchase the right to occupy the coveted seats.

The multimillion-dollar advertising campaign thrilled fans with anticipation worldwide, from Australia to Korea to France. Lavish trailers designed to tantalize the emotions and lure entertainment seekers revealed morsels of the plot's prophecy: "A fire will rise" splashed across the screen, throngs of people eerily chanting, and a scene where Catwoman whispers to Batman's alter-ego, "There's a storm coming, Mr. Wayne."[6]

In spite of a caution that children ages thirteen and under should not see the movie, fans brought children as young as five years old and filled an Aurora, Colorado, theater, ecstatic to attend the midnight premiere of the predicted blockbuster film.

While the audience was captivated by the high-tech drama and powerful violence, a twenty-four-year-old man slipped into the theater wearing a gas mask and tactical gear. Moviegoers who noticed him thought he was part of a publicity stunt to promote the film. Instead, a premeditated attack began with tear gas followed by dispersing ammunition into the audience of eyewitnesses. Within minutes chaos turned to carnage, and the theater became a sinister crime scene.[7]

When the raid ceased, the perpetrator disappeared from the theater. When captured, he introduced himself as the Joker.[8] He certainly had not entertained the crowd as the villains in the trilogy of films had; rather, he had executed a hideous plan with precision, leaving victims screaming, groaning, or dead.

The film continued to flash across the big screen, but spectators were no longer looking for Batman to come back and save the imaginary city. Those who had ducked underneath the seats were terrified of the masked sniper. Some moaned whispers, "Do you think he's coming back?" In the aftermath survivors bellowed that the dark night had risen—indeed. A woman who later recounted the massacre said, "I came thinking that good would win over evil, but evil has triumphed again. I will always be on the lookout for evil that lurks in the darkness."[9]

The Unease of Our Time

Reports were chilling as pop culture was unmasked. Observers wondered why spectators flock to entertainment that feeds fear and deposits caustic thoughts into unstable minds. Could it be for the reason one woman revealed why she and her family frequent such films? She stated that she believes it is *fun* to be in a large auditorium where everyone is screaming in "holy terror." During the conversation, she also pointed out, "It's a rare moment that seems to bring strangers together because the panic from the big screen affects everyone the same." Fans in Aurora had stepped into a virtual world before midnight, but they discovered that the dark night brought unwelcomed reality and untold pain.

Christopher Nolan also released a statement in which he said, "Watching a story unfold on screen is an important and joyful pastime. . . . The idea that someone would violate that innocent and hopeful place in such an unbearably savage way is devastating."[10] He didn't mention the fact that such savagery had been orchestrated and promoted for worldwide pleasure. One could ask, "How can violence ever be a joyful pastime?"

An *Entertainment Weekly* reporter surprisingly wrote,

> The Dark Knight [trilogy] has captured the unease of our times—the post-traumatic stress of so much catastrophe, the ominous dread that there's more and maybe worse to come; the worry (and denial) that we're handling the whole thing wrong and becoming worse for it. . . . I'm ready to leave the dark night behind and make a better, truer future.[11]

Everywhere, people seemed to be asking, "Is there any hope that society can be changed?"

I was struck by these sentiments because of the resentment people have to the message of the Bible that predicts a storm is coming. A fire will rise; the final war between good and evil will take place, and good—not evil—will triumph. Why do people accept violence from the world as entertainment and pay good money to be scared to death by Hollywood while at the same time curse the Christian message of truth, which warns of evil and offers refuge from the terrorist of the soul?

The same people who say that preachers frighten them with such violence are not listening to the antidote. You see, there *is* hope for the hearts of mankind to be changed.

HOPE AND CHANGE

Are we ready for hope and change? Most would say yes. That idea captured a nation and ushered in a new American president in 2008. Four years later citizens returned to the polls despite their dashed hopes, and the president was reelected; but the world had not found the hope it sought, though there had been change.

Hopelessness abounded. News outlets such as the BBC, Al Jazeera, NPR, CNN, and even Facebook ran articles about "Hope and Change in Israel."

Headlines announced a "Coalition for Hope and Change in Afghanistan." War continues.

"Is There Any Hope for Change in Sudan?" Christians are still under attack.

"Iraqis Hope for Change." Things don't look good.

One headline writer offered a glimmer of hope—"How to Make Hope and Change Happen"—but the article offered no solutions.

Few are finding hope as revealed in these stories: "Young People Lose Hope in Asia," "No Change—Dwindling Hope" (in the Middle East), and "Why Hope and Change Is Dead" (in America). The articles don't leave readers much hope for change. But one headline writer posed a worthy question: Are we "Looking for Hope in All the Wrong Places"?

Hope seems a rare commodity in our society today. Hoping in science, education, social programs, and government has proven hollow. We've grasped the fringe of technology, bringing instant messaging and global communication, but technology has also given us nuclear warheads to destroy those with whom we communicate.

Back in 1968, John W. Gardner, US secretary of health, education and welfare under President Lyndon Johnson, stated,

> More and more [people] feel threatened by runaway technology, by large-scale organizations, by overcrowding. More and more . . . are appalled by the ravages of industrial progress, by the defacement of nature, by man-made ugliness. If our society continues at its present rate to become less livable as it becomes more affluent, we promise all to end up in sumptuous misery.[12]

Almost fifty years later people are still restless, still hopeless, and in utter despair.

So where do we place our hope? What do we want changed? Who can fulfill our hopes? And how can anyone bring about change that will make this world better? I can tell you that no one belonging to the human race is capable. The flaw in human nature is too great. Humanity's lofty ideas at best fall short.

Socialist and communist regimes attempt to spread oppression beyond their borders while their people dream of fleeing tyranny; these people want change, they want freedom. Sharia-governed nations want to change the world with their brand of repression while their people silently hope to escape their cloistered existence.

People who oppose change are often ridiculed while those who campaign for change are celebrated. But the objective of change is the key. When someone exchanges right for wrong, change becomes a wicked agent.

Few would disagree that the world has benefitted from changing our modes of transportation—replacing horses with automobiles and exchanging passenger ships for planes—or replacing oil lamps with electricity. While some countries have won freedom from bondage, others are in danger of exchanging freedom for bondage. We have seen freedom of speech give license to spewing hate and tolerance skewing right and wrong. We take pride in having freedom, but freedom in what? Some freedom-lovers value laws based on moral standards while others fight for laws that uphold the debasement of immorality. Some want to change what God has defined as evil and define it as good. Change can be good; it can also be very bad.

It is, therefore, stunning to consider that those who have enjoyed liberty to live and worship freely are dropping an anchor of hope in other human beings who promise change for the better but who can't deliver. Some harness freedom and open the floodgates of chaos. Still people clamor for hope and change, blinded to evil disguised as good. When people begin saying that "hope is an ugly four-letter word," we have a glimpse into the desperation of the human heart. Clearly hope and change according to the world's definitions are not the answers.

Harvard graduate and Pulitzer Prize–winning columnist Walter Lippmann once stated: "For us all the world is disorderly and dangerous, ungoverned and apparently ungovernable."[13] Lippmann died in 1974, but his words still seem apt. Who alone can overcome the danger of evil and restore order? Who alone can govern the world?

The answer will come out of Heaven on the clouds of glory when the holy One steps out from the throne room of Heaven and brings victorious change to this weary and wicked world. The God of hope will speak the word, sending His Son once more from Heaven to earth; for this is the fulfillment of His whole word to the whole world. He is the only Change Agent who transforms man's nature by changing his source of hope. But only those who have acknowledged this truth and accepted it will recognize Him on the great day that He comes again.

Who is this Man of hope? His name is Jesus Christ. Hope rests in God's Son alone, not in the affairs or the change agents of this world.

True hope and real change is coming to this world. No government can prevent it, no individual can escape it, and those who refuse to embrace its reality will never change its certainty. The end of the world as we know it will take place when Christ returns to earth. It is a doomsday prediction for scoffers who refuse to believe, but it is a glorious prospect for those who know He is coming again.

Jesus Christ will one day come back in great glory—as King. Are you looking for Him?

Optimism Can Kill You

Admiral Jim Stockdale was one of the highest-ranking officers in the US Navy, served in Vietnam, and spent time as a prisoner of war in the infamous "Hanoi Hilton." He once was asked which men did not make it out of the war prison. His answer was surprising: "The optimists." He went on to explain. "You must never confuse faith that you will prevail in the end—which you can never afford to lose—with the discipline to confront the most brutal facts of your current reality."[14]

This is what Scripture teaches. We cannot take ourselves off the hook by hoping that we will escape God's judgment without confronting the brutal fact of sin and dealing with its reality. Sin is a killer, and sin will be massacred in the Day of Judgment. Jesus said,

Nation will rise against nation, and kingdom against kingdom. And there will be famines, pestilences, and earthquakes in various places. All these are the beginning of sorrows. . . .

And then many will be offended, will betray one another, and will hate one another. . . . Because lawlessness will abound, the love of many will grow cold. But he who endures to the end shall be saved. And this gospel of the kingdom will be preached in all the world as a witness to all the nations, and then the end will come. (Matthew 24:7–8, 10, 12–14)

Truth is not always pleasant, but truth is always absolute. When optimism ignores truth, the reality of hope dies.

Four-Letter Words: *Hope* and *Love*

The truth about hope in God is found in His glorious Gospel, the Good News of salvation, motivated by the most magnificent four-letter word—*love*. True love will always sound the alarm and point to the way of escape. The attributes of God cannot be fathomed, but they are to be followed. The Bible says that God is "kind to the unthankful and evil" (Luke 6:35).

So how can God stand by and allow people to die in their sin, you may ask? He didn't stand by; He sent His Son to the cross. He doesn't stand by today and turn His face from sinners; He extends His long arm of salvation. Will you reach out and take what He lovingly offers? Are you considering Him?

Scripture is relentless in confirming the patience of God, but a time will come when He says, "Enough!" The Bible says, "The hearts of the sons of men are full of evil; madness is in their hearts while they live" (Ecclesiastes 9:3). This is revealed every day around the world and certainly in America, a nation whose foundation was built upon the principlal truths of Almighty God. My wife, Ruth, once said, "If God doesn't punish America, He'll have to apologize to Sodom and Gomorrah."

Not long ago when the most precious human institution—marriage—came under brutal attack in my home state of North Carolina, I wondered what Ruth would think of America if she were alive today. In the few short years that she's been gone, our nation has wandered further down the moral ladder. Millions of babies have been aborted while the government pays money we don't have to save the whales. We are outraged at violence, one against another, while we pay money to be entertained by glorifying violence.

Society strives to avoid any possibility of offending anyone—except God. Yet the further we get from God, the more America and, yes, the whole world spirals out of control. Self-centered indulgence, pride, and a lack of shame over sin are our own emblems of a pop-culture lifestyle. My heart aches for the nations and its deceived people.

There was a time when other nations looked up to the United States and desired to emulate what made America great. It wasn't prosperity and living the American dream that made America great but reverence for God and living according to His Word. The results were untold blessings. God used America to spread the Gospel to the world. Now we see many of its citizens shaking their fists in the face of Almighty God.

How can we escape our own sin-inflicted darkness? How can we rise from the dark night and change from bleak existence into the light of hope for a better life?

The answers to these questions are found in God's Word. But within the answers is the reality that a day of doom is coming for many. It is not a fictional tale. It is a faithful truth. The Bible tells us that Jesus is coming back in great glory. Are you expecting Him?

He is not a caped crusader—He is the crucified Christ. He is not a superhero who falters—He is the Savior who rescues. He is not make-believe—He is Master. He is not a legend—He is Lord. He isn't created by fantasy—He is favored by God. He is not an icon—He is the Intercessor. He is not a force—He is the Forgiver. He is not imaginary—He is infallible. He does not vanish into exile—He redeems to the end. He is not a virtual winner—He is the Victor. He does not resemble hope—He is the resurrection of Hope. He is not a revolutionary—He is the Righteous Ruler. He is not a knight in hiding—He is the coming King.

The Bible speaks the truth about the dark side of human nature and the dark future of those who refuse God's offer of salvation. I would not be honest with you if I just told you the happy ending. The truth is that there will be a glorious ending, but we cannot ignore the Bible's warning that a day is coming when sin will have its final judgment.

THE DARK KNIGHT OR THE COMING KING

God does not leave us alone to wallow in this terrorized reality. How do I know? The Bible tells us that Christ the risen One is coming back someday very soon. His name is Jesus, and He will conquer the dark knight of evil—his name is Satan. This is the true story of good versus evil. It is real. The Victor and the villain will be embroiled in battle. And the outcome is certain: King Jesus will overcome the evil one. The villain with all of his vileness will be bound in the bowels of obscurity. His dominion will be cast down for eternity. My friend, this is good news—this is real hope.

The Lord Jesus is the God of mercy, and He responds to repentance. We see this in the biblical account of Nineveh, the lone world super-power of its day—wealthy, unconcerned, self-centered . . . and targeted for divine destruction. But when the reluctant prophet Jonah finally heeded God, traveled to Nineveh, and proclaimed God's warning, people heard and repented. Nineveh was saved.

Now the questions for those who are estranged from this merciful God are: Will you ally yourself with the villain and follow him to the place of eternal judgment, or will you distinguish yourself as belonging to the Overcomer, the Lord Jesus Christ? Will you confess that you are done with the dark night and come into the light of His salvation? Will you rise to the heights of the King's glory or sink into the dark night of eternal condemnation?

Some may say, "You're frightening me!" If you were given the opportunity to meet a king, would you refuse the invitation out of fear? Or would you rush to put on your finest garment and wait patiently for an audience with royalty? The answer is found in whether or not you are received by the king as his ally or his rival. If you have obeyed the king, you will anticipate being in his presence. If you know that you have come against the king, you will be in terror of standing before him.

We see the world kicking God out of education, government, marriages, the home, and even church. Yet when terror strikes, people clasp their hands and bend their knees, calling on God to meet them in their time of distress, asking Him to lift their burden, begging for a different outcome.

Here is God's message to you: "Come to Me. . . . Learn from Me, for I am gentle and lowly in heart, and you will find rest for your souls. For My yoke is easy and My burden is light" (Matthew 11:28–30). Don't wait for tragedy to strike before you turn to Him. He is waiting for you to come to Him now. Don't wait for the day of doom—it will be too late. When you come to Him, you must remain with Him.

My friend, we will all stand before the great and mighty King of Heaven one day. The Bible gives us this wonderful hope. You do not have to live in dread of this coming event. The Bible tells of judgment coming to those who have rejected Christ, but it also makes it clear that those who have received Him should anticipate the moment of His return with thrilling wonder.

This is the reason for Scripture's repeated warning: "Prepare to meet your God" (Amos 4:12; also see Matthew 24:44 and 1 John 2:28). What a marvelous command. What a glorious hope.

THE LOVING WARNING FROM GOD

This was the message from the weeping prophet, Jeremiah, in the Old Testament. He was known as the doomsday prophet, called to warn the people that judgment would come if they didn't repent. The Israelites refused to heed God's warning that they must turn from their sinful ways. Not even his family believed his message from God; he felt terribly alone.

Jeremiah knew, however, the faithful love that prompted the Lord to command that people repent of their wickedness. Boldly he proclaimed: "Thus says the LORD, 'Behold, I am fashioning a disaster and devising a plan against you. Return now every one from his evil way, and make your ways and your doings good'" (Jeremiah 18:11).

Let me emphasize that this is a hopeful message. God's warnings are always fortified with hope. Aren't you thankful when the fire alarm sounds, giving the opportunity to douse the flames or escape a blaze that is out of control? Aren't you relieved to hear a siren when you're in trouble and know that help is on its way? If your ship begins to sink, will you refuse to board the lifeboat? The Bible has given us fair warning and shown us the way of escape. Will you heed the sirens' sounding, or will you scoff at Heaven's call?

Jeremiah was sounding the alarm that a storm was brewing, shouting the way of escape. But the people ignored Jeremiah. They scoffed at the holy Word of God. Because of the people's extreme love for evil, because of their salacious appetite for wickedness, they willingly rebelled and replied, "We will walk according to our own plans, and we will every one obey the dictates of his evil heart" (Jeremiah 18:12). Doesn't this sound familiar today?

Distraught by the coming night of darkness, Jeremiah had prayed to God,

> You are my hope in the day of doom.
> Let them be ashamed who persecute me. . . .
> Let them be dismayed. . . .
> Bring on them the day of doom,
> And destroy them with double destruction!
>
> (JEREMIAH 17:17–18)

And how did the Lord respond to His servant Jeremiah? He exhibited patience and commanded Jeremiah to continue proclaiming God's urgent message: "Go and stand in the gate . . . and say . . . 'Hear the word of the LORD'" (vv. 19–20), giving the people warning to "take heed to yourselves" (v. 21). Sadly, they still "did not obey nor incline their ear, but made their neck stiff, that they might not hear nor receive instruction" (v. 23). And the destruction Jeremiah predicted did come to pass.

This was certainly not the first or last time God spoke about the day of doom. His compassionate warnings provide a way of escape, a way to salvation. And His warnings are most often followed by promises full of hope. Are you heeding the warning or grasping for another way? My friend, God's way is the right way—it is the only way.

ESCAPING FLOODS AND FIRE

We see this in the epic story of Noah, perhaps the most unlikely seaman in the history of the world. Jesus spoke of Noah, who was the first in the Bible to be called a righteous man. Jesus was predicting that a dark night was coming and equated this warning with the one God gave to the people of Noah's day—destruction is coming once again to earth.

There will be great tribulation, such as has not been since the beginning of the world. . . .

Immediately after the tribulation of those days the sun will be darkened, and the moon will not give its light; the stars will fall from heaven, and the powers of the heavens will be shaken. . . . All the tribes of the earth will mourn, and they will see the Son of Man coming on the clouds of heaven with power and great glory. . . .

But as the days of Noah were, so also will the coming of the Son of Man be. For as in the days before the flood, they were eating and drinking, marrying and giving in marriage, until the day that Noah entered the ark, and did not know until the flood came and took them all away, so also will the coming of the Son of Man be. . . .

Therefore you also be ready, for the Son of Man is coming at an hour you do not expect. (Matthew 24:21, 29–30, 37–39, 44)

Peter also wrote about the days of Noah:

Be mindful of the words which were spoken . . . by the holy prophets . . . knowing this first: that scoffers will come in the last days, walking according to their own lusts, and saying, "Where is the promise of His coming? For since the fathers fell asleep, all things continue as they were from the beginning of creation." For this they willfully forget: that by the word of God the heavens were of old, and the earth standing out of water and in the water, by which the world that then existed perished, being flooded with water. But the heavens and the earth which are now preserved by the same word, are reserved for fire until the day of judgment. . . .

The Lord is not slack concerning His promise . . . but is longsuffering toward us, not willing that any should perish but that all should come to repentance. (2 Peter 3:2–7, 9)

The earth was destroyed by water before Christ's first coming; and it will be destroyed again by fire at Christ's second coming—but it will also be cleansed. Fire can destroy, but fire also purifies. We see God's message reflected in floodwaters that submerged the earth in the early chapters of Scripture, and we can almost feel the fervent heat spoken of in the last books of the Bible; flames that will engulf the earth, dissolving its elements, making provision for the fulfillment of promise.

What miner who discovers gold does not put it through the refiner's fire to uncover its worth? God is the Master Miner and Refiner. The earth belongs to Him, but human sin has polluted it. He is coming back to reclaim what is rightfully His and has invited those whose sin has been cleansed to reign with Him in a new Heaven and a new earth.

Do you see the reflection of God's purity in the promised flames? He will not dwell on a sin-infested planet. He will strike it with fire that will burn away the dross. He will restore humanity and its dwelling to the pristine condition that was in the beginning. For those who believe in Him, there is no reason to fear the end because the end is the new beginning. This is very good news; it is God's message of great hope to the world.

The human heart does not change without Christ transforming it. For those who believe they can be good without repentance from total depravity, without humbling themselves before Jesus Christ, who redeems fallen humanity, they are engaged in folly, just as in the days of Noah:

> Then the LORD saw that the wickedness of man was great in the earth, and that every intent of the thoughts of his heart was only evil continually. And the LORD . . . was grieved in His heart. . . .
>
> God looked upon the earth, and indeed it was corrupt; for all flesh had corrupted their way on the earth. (Genesis 6:5–6, 12)

But thank God there was a man who found grace in the eyes of the Lord. Only eight souls—Noah and his family—survived the greatest catastrophe the world has ever known. The story of the great Flood occurred when the days of Noah were filled with violence. People loved sin—they idolized sin; they were immersed in sin. The flood was not a natural catastrophe but a moral one. It was God's judgment on people's disbelief in God, reflected in their attitudes and actions. So God set a time limit, warning people to change (repent of sin) or be swept away in a drowning flood. But His warning was not without hope. How do I know? God told Noah to build an ark.

The Bible teaches from cover to cover that judgment is coming. But even in God's judgment His love is dominant and His patience protracted. And He never gives warning without providing hope for those who will listen.

There are many still today who reject God based on the story of Noah alone. Why should this surprise us? The entire population, except eight souls, scoffed at Noah as he preached that judgment was coming. Not much has changed. The world is still scoffing at those who proclaim God's warning that judgment is on its way but everlasting peace will follow. Don't fail to see the warning and the promise.

In 2012, even in the midst of one of the most heated election seasons in American history, we saw the display of multiple thousands of citizens demanding that God be removed from the national political scene. They did not want to be aligned with "In God We Trust." They apparently would rather trust in flawed people who have no control over tomorrow.

Only through a deep abiding faith in what cannot be seen is it possible to trust in God. The scorn of others can be a powerful explosive on a person's faith in God if it is not empowered by His absolute truth.

Consider Noah. God did. The Bible says, "Noah found grace in the eyes of the LORD" (Genesis 6:8).

THE HUNDRED-YEAR WARNING

Can you imagine what the people thought when Noah began chopping down trees and building an enormous ark on dry land, far from any ocean? Noah knew nothing about sailing the high seas, and he certainly was at a loss as to how to build a boat, even with God's detailed instructions. But he believed God when He said it would rain and the land would flood, in spite of the fact that it had never rained upon the earth. Still, over a hundred-year period, Noah faithfully carried out God's command. Noah's faith defied all human rationale. Through his obedience, he exhibited faith in God and was called righteous.

This monumental assignment from Heaven surely required Noah to hire workers to carry out God's command. These men must have thought their work was without purpose. Perhaps they had faith in their work to build a vessel of safety but didn't have enough faith to heed the warning to climb aboard before water began falling from the heavens.

But Noah believed God by faith in "the evidence of things not seen" (Hebrews 11:1). That is authentic faith. He so revered God that he prepared the ark "for the saving of his household, by which he condemned the world and became heir of the righteousness which is according to faith" (v. 7). Would you commit yourself to an ark of salvation while it sits on dry land?

I am so thankful that Noah and his family trusted the Master of the sea and the Captain of the ship. Noah kept his eyes on God, and God gave him the strength to endure rejection, truth to rebuke the world, and faith to receive God's righteousness. How marvelous is God's patience with us. God had extended His love, righteousness, and mercy to the people of Noah's day in every possible way. They rejected it all.

It is hard to fathom what went through Noah's mind as he walked up the plank and entered the only door to the ark. As a preacher, I can't comprehend preaching for one hundred twenty years, as Noah did, with no converts. A waterfall of tears must have washed down his face as he felt the waves lift the boat that swiftly carried him away from a world that had turned its back on the repeated warning.

Were the people still ridiculing Noah and laughing at him as he sailed away, or did Noah hear the gut-wrenching cries as the waters deepened and people struggled to reach the ark of safety? Either way, it was too late. The people had settled for the world they loved and died in the restless waves of their choosing.

Today those who rebuke the world for its immorality and injustice are considered intolerant, but God's warning is a rebuke on man's sin, and His salvation will not be granted to those who continue in it. Here in the early pages of Scripture, we see the reality of sin and God's great invitation to flee from it and "come into the ark" (Genesis 7:1). We see the tremendous hope that God grants. This is the first time Scripture uses the word *come,* and it reveals the heart of a saving God. All through Scripture we hear this welcoming word. *Come!*

God had told Noah to make a window for the ark for light and only one door to enter in. Do not miss the symbolism of this marvelous picture. Christ is the ark of salvation. He is the Light of the World. And Jesus also said, "I am the door" (John 10:9)—the only way to salvation.

Just imagine being aboard the ark during a forty-day monsoon and riding the surges and breakers for months before feeling the boat rest on dry land. Over the course of a year or more, Noah's family of eight experienced the faithfulness of God's protection, realized the fulfillment of God's prophecy, and then beheld the favor of God's promise—a rainbow—to signify that the earth would never again be destroyed by water.

We today have the advantage of looking back in history on what was to come and did come to pass, yet we turn a blind eye to what is happening and a deaf ear to warnings of what is yet to happen. A British reporter has said, "The world is on a collision course with disaster."[15]

His Coming Is Hope

Today the only bright spot on the horizon is the promise of the coming again of Christ. This is God's message, and this is the message that Christ's church is commanded to proclaim. The church is not bound in a building or in a denomination. The church—represented by the people of God—has been given the task of sounding the alarm for humanity to repent and turn from the sin that reigns in human hearts, just as Noah did in ancient days.

God keeps His promises, and this is why we can be sure that the return of Christ is near. Scripture tells us that there will be signs pointing toward the return of the Lord. I believe all of these signs are evident today. Those who refuse to repent have no hope. They live in fear of what will happen when life as we know it comes to an end. For them, the second coming of Christ is doomsday preaching. But for those who have put their hope in the Savior of the world, the future shines as an ever-brightening beam in a darkening world. This is not fanciful imagination, but the clear and repeated testimony of the Bible.

What a time to take the news of the day in one hand and the Bible in the other and watch the unfolding of the great drama of the ages come together. This is an exciting and thrilling time to be alive. I would not want to live in any other period. The Apocalypse (the unveiling of the end times) speaks powerfully of trouble ahead with storm warnings that carry a booming jolt of truth. The warning is clear: prepare to meet thy God—followed by the voice of the gentle Shepherd—"Come."

A new world is coming. The paradise that man lost will be regained. One day we will live in a brand-new world. Someday Christ will come again to conquer evil and establish His perfect rule over all creation. But until then God wants to give everyone an opportunity to know Christ through repentance and faith. Regardless of what society says, we can't go on much longer in the sea of immorality without judgment coming. We are at a crossroads, and there are profound moral issues at stake. It is time to return to biblical truth.

The book of Matthew clearly speaks of coming judgment in a ninety-seven-verse profile of what the world will look like before Jesus' return to earth (Matthew 24–25). We see Jesus as King who will come back and remake the world and establish His kingdom. Do you know the King?

While Jesus walked on earth, He preached the Gospel of the kingdom of God. This is a message that even the church sometimes fails to preach, yet it answers the questions that are on people's minds today: Is the end of the world coming soon? Will the earth be destroyed? What is our fate? The world says this is all a great mystery, but the Bible tells us with certainty that Jesus is coming again to bring an end to the human experience and usher in a glorious eternity for those who stand with Him. The Bible says, "The day of the LORD is coming" (Zechariah 14:1). He is the coming King, and there is a heavenly kingdom coming. Are you prepared for the end times?

The late Dr. S. M. Lockridge, who addressed the Billy Graham School of Evangelism on several occasions, recorded a video tribute to Jesus Christ, the King of kings. It is worth seeing. This remarkable bit of preaching was combined with images, and the resulting video went viral on YouTube. It beautifully captures the enthusiasm of those who *know* Jesus is coming again. I love what he said. "Do you know Him? . . . You can't outlive Him, and you can't live without Him. . . . That's my King!"[16]

When God spoke to the prophet Isaiah about the coming salvation, He told him to write down everything he heard,

> that it may be for the time to come
> as a witness forever.
>
> (ISAIAH 30:8 ESV)

He added,

> Therefore the LORD waits to be gracious to you. . . .
> blessed are all those who wait for him.
>
> (v. 18 ESV)

Christ's coming again is mentioned all through Scripture. We are told that the world will one day acknowledge that Jesus Christ is Lord (Philippians 2:10–11), that Jesus will sit on the throne (Luke 1:32), and that there will be universal joy among the redeemed (Isaiah 51:11).

What can we do to prepare for this great day? Believe in Him who makes your salvation sure. Rest in hope that He is purifying you (1 John 3:3). Desire His imminent return. Wait patiently for the promise to be fulfilled (Hebrews 11:9–10). Watch in faith for His coming again (Hebrews 11:13). Look for this blessed hope (Titus 2:13).

The Bible tells us that the state of the world will grow darker as we near the end of the age. This is evident when we hear even secular news reporters from many of the major networks make statements such as "The world has gone nuts," or ask questions such as "What is the world coming to?"

The book of Revelation gives us the answers, and while many feel that it is difficult and demanding to read, it is the only biblical book whose author promises a blessing to those who read it. The end of the world as we know it will culminate with Jesus Christ coming again as the King triumphant.

I am deeply aware of the enormous problems that face our world today and the dangerous trends that seem to be leading our world to the brink of Armageddon. The "god of this age" (2 Corinthians 4:4) has blinded the minds of those who do not believe so that the light of the Gospel of the Lord Jesus Christ will have no impact. The Bible tells us that the Antichrist will take the world by storm, promising prosperity and peace. His popularity will lure hearts and deceive minds. The human race will be caught up in exhilaration, believing the Antichrist alone will solve their dilemmas and bring global tranquility. This is why the Bible warns, "Be saved from this perverse generation" (Acts 2:40). But when the King of glory breaks through the storm clouds, He will reveal to the world the great deceiver and gather to Himself all those who belong to Him.

Nothing is taking God by surprise, nor should it catch us unaware. This string of events has been foretold in the pages of Scripture. History speaks of it, and history is being made as the world moves rapidly toward the climax when God's Son, Jesus Christ, returns as the rightful Ruler of the world.

It is not just Christians that sense something is about to happen. The world knows that things cannot go on as they are. History has reached an impasse. This world is on a collision course. Something is about to give. With increasing frequency, commentators from secular media speak of Armageddon. *The Telegraph* in Great Britain ran an article, "Doomsday

Clock ticks one minute closer to Armageddon."[17] A Fox News headline speaks of "Taking the pulse of Armageddon."[18] While reporters speculate on the timetable and attempt to decipher the signs, the truth is that no one but God Himself knows when that time will come. But it will come!

This strikes many people with great fear, but fear can be overcome by faith in God. Remember that while the Bible sounds the alarm and warns mankind to prepare, the Bible also predicts a fabulous future for those who trust in Him. He who does all things well will bring beauty from the ashes of world chaos. A new world will be born. A new social order will emerge when Christ comes back. A fabulous future is on the way. The second coming of Christ will be so revolutionary that it will change every aspect of life on this planet. Christ will reign in righteousness. Disease will be eliminated. Death will be abolished. War will be eradicated. Nature will be transformed. Men, women, and children will live as life was originally designed, in fellowship with God and each other.

Does this give you hope for real change? If not, I urge you to examine where you stand before the God of judgment, but with the certain hope that He is the same God of peace.

Someone once observed that there are three days a week that we have no control over—yesterday, today, and tomorrow. We only have this moment in time to prepare for eternity. For those who delay, why do you wait? If you think you can clean up your past to make preparation feasible, your efforts are futile. You can't change your past, but you can change your future.

MY HOPE

Perhaps you have read this book out of curiosity. Maybe you have turned each page looking for inspiration. It is even possible you have studied each word, searching for answers. My hope is that the message you have read in this book will drive you to God's Book, which holds the key to hope for tomorrow—eternal life—and that you will have the certainty of knowing that your future will be secure in the promises of eternal hope found only in the Lord and Savior Jesus Christ.

You see, one glorious day the Lord Jesus is going to open the Book of Life and He will read the names of the redeemed. "Anyone not found written in the Book of Life" will be "cast into the lake of fire" (Revelation 20:15). Do you know the voice of the Savior? Will you hear Him call your name?

I will hear Him call my name not because I have preached for more than seventy years. Not because I have done anything good. I will hear my name because His sheep hear His voice (John 10:27). The Lord Jesus has heard my confession of sin, my acknowledgment of need, and He reached down and saved me. He purchased my soul with His blood.

What about you? Is your name written in the Book of Life? Do you long to hear Him call you by name? Are you ready for the dark night to end? Are you ready for a new day, a new world, a new way of life? Are you ready for God's provision of true hope and real change?

There is coming a day of greater conflict than the world has ever known. Those who belong to Jesus Christ will endure persecution with hope, knowing that God's righteousness will be victorious over the embattlement of sin. Where do you stand on the battlefield of good versus evil?

Friend, I can tell you that if you belong to the King of Heaven you will be victorious when the end of time as we know it comes. I have read the last page of the Bible. If you know Him, everything's going to turn out all right. Jesus, the changeless One whose promises never change (Malachi 3:6), will break through the dark night and rise as the conquering Champion and reigning King of glory.

The psalmist declared,

> The earth is the LORD's, and all its fullness. . . .
> For He has founded it upon the seas,
> And established it upon the waters. . . .
> Who may stand in His holy place?

He who has clean hands and a pure heart,
Who has not lifted up his soul to an idol,
Nor sworn deceitfully.
He shall receive blessing from the LORD,
And righteousness from the God of his salvation. . . .
Lift up your heads. . . .
And the King of glory shall come in.
Who is this King of glory?
The LORD strong and mighty,
The LORD mighty in battle. . . .
He is the King of glory.

(PSALM 24)

In the last book of the Bible, Jesus declares, "Behold, I am coming quickly! Blessed is he who keeps the words of the prophecy of this book" (Revelation 22:7).

Do you think He is coming back? I don't think it; I *know* He's coming back—and soon. THIS IS MY HOPE.

Looking for the blessed hope and glorious appearing
of our great God and Savior Jesus Christ, who gave
Himself for us, that He might redeem us.
(TITUS 2:13–14)

AFTERWORD

LIVING LIFE
WITH HOPE

S PEAKING TO STUDENTS ON COLLEGE AND UNIVERSITY
CAMPUSES HAS ALWAYS BEEN A GREAT PRIVILEGE FOR
ME. Young people by nature are truth seekers, but many often get
bogged down by theoretical ideals that hinder truth. I can recall being
approached by a sophomore who asked, "Mr. Graham, you won't let us
down, will you?" Puzzled, I asked him what he meant. He explained,
"Please tell us how to find God. That's what we need."

On another campus a student said, "Mr. Graham, we hear a lot about
what Christ has done for us, the value of religion, and what personal
salvation is. But nobody tells us how to find Christ."

This lament of an honest student became a challenge to me to explain
simply and plainly how to find Christ. This is the critical and clear message
of Scripture, and it is my desire to proclaim its life-changing truth.

God has made the plan of redemption plain. Finding Jesus Christ
and having the assurance of His salvation is essential to securing eternal
life with Him in Heaven.

First, you must be convinced that you need Him. If you feel that you
are self-sufficient, capable of meeting life head-on and under your own
power, then you will never find Him. A reading of the Gospels will reveal

that Jesus did not impose Himself upon those who felt self-sufficient, righteous, and self-confident.

There must be recognition of your own sinfulness and spiritual need before there can be a response from Christ. He came to call not the righteous but sinners to repentance. Many divine promises hinge on a condition: "*If* we walk in the light . . . the blood of Jesus Christ His Son cleanses us from all sin. . . . *If* we confess our sins, He is faithful and just to forgive us our sins and to cleanse us from all unrighteousness" (1 John 1:7, 9, italics added).

Second, you must understand the message of the cross. Many great theologians have never understood the mysteries of the cross. Many intellectuals have made up theories as to why Christ died and the eternal significance of His death. None of the theories seem to satisfy. The Bible says that the natural man cannot comprehend the things of God, so how can people understand the cross before they find Christian assurance? It is only when we understand that Christ died in the place of sinners, for sin, that we find the elements of satisfaction.

Here is where the miracle lies. Just as the apostle Peter by a divine revelation said, "You are the Christ, the Son of the living God" (Matthew 16:16), so by a miracle the meaning of the cross will be given to you by the Holy Spirit of God.

I remember a young reporter in Glasgow who attended our meetings at Kelvin Hall as part of his assignment. He heard the Gospel night after night, but it seemed to make no impact upon him.

One day, however, a colleague asked him, "What are they preaching down there?" He tried to explain the Gospel he had heard, and in so doing, he found himself saying, "You see, it's this way. Christ died for me. . . . Christ died for my sins." And when he said that, he suddenly realized the words were true! The full meaning of the message burst in miraculously upon him, and then and there he received salvation by acknowledging his sin, receiving Christ's work on the cross for the forgiveness of his sin, and committing himself wholly to Jesus Christ.

How vivid, how alive, the cross becomes when the apostle Paul speaks of it: "I have been crucified with Christ; it is no longer I who live, but Christ lives in me" (Galatians 2:20). When you see Him high and lifted up—the Son of God smitten, marred, bruised, and dying for you—and understand that He loved you and gave Himself for you, you will have taken the second step toward the Christian's assurance of salvation.

Third, as you have read, you must count the cost. This is what I explained to one of the students seeking truth. It is important to note that Jesus discouraged superficial enthusiasm. He urged people to consider the cost of being His disciple: "If anyone desires to come after Me, let him deny himself, and take up his cross daily, and follow Me" (Luke 9:23). Jesus said, "Count the cost . . . whoever of you does not forsake all that he has cannot be My disciple" (Luke 14:28, 33).

Like the rich young ruler of old, the student who asked how to find God went away sad. He did count the cost and was not willing to pay the price of openly acknowledging Jesus Christ as his Savior. Rather, he counted his self-sufficiency more valuable than dependence upon the Lord.

Fourth, you must confess Jesus Christ as Lord of your life. I have always asked people to make this public confession in our meetings because Jesus in His earthly ministry demanded a definite commitment. He had reasons for demanding that people openly follow Him. Jesus knew that an unwitnessed vow is no vow at all. Until you have surrendered to Christ by a conscious act of your will, you are not a Christian.

Have you taken this definite step? The Bible says, "As many as received Him, to them He gave the right to become children of God, to those who believe in His name" (John 1:12).

Fifth, you must be willing for God to change your life. When you come to Christ, you are considered a spiritual baby. As you read the New Testament, you will see how the early disciples, during the first days of following Christ, faltered and often failed. They quarreled, they were envious, they were contentious, they were unfaithful, and they often grew angry.

However, as they became emptied of self and filled with Christ, they developed into the fullness of the stature of a Christian. This is what Christ empowers you to do as you walk in new life with Him.

Many struggle because they want Christ to walk with them, but believers are instructed to leave their own pathways and walk with Christ. He comes in and saves us, and then we place ourselves completely in Him. Conversion is the first step to this wonderful new journey. A new life begins the moment you receive Christ and the Holy Spirit takes up residence. During the rest of your lifetime, God will be busy conforming you to the image of His Son, the Lord Jesus Christ. This is "the mystery which has been hidden from ages and from generations, but now has been revealed to His saints. To them God willed to make known what are the riches of the glory of this mystery . . . which is Christ in you, the hope of glory . . . which works in me mightily" (Colossians 1:26–27, 29).

Part of counting the cost is realizing that when this transformation takes place, you will become a target of Satan, who is the enemy of Christ. When you walk Satan's way in the world, he doesn't go out of his way to bother you. He has you; you are his child. But when you become a Christian, a child of God, Satan will use all of his diabolical techniques to thwart, hinder, and defeat you. Have you considered the cost?

Sixth, when you are saved you must desire nourishment from God's Word. Be faithful in reading the Bible, praying for God's guidance and strength each day, seeking the fellowship of other believers as part of Christ's church, and sharing your new faith with those who are still wandering in darkness. The church is the Body of Christ on earth, and it is important to join with other followers of Jesus Christ to learn from one another and to encourage one another.

I cannot imagine living in a world without other believers. In all of my travels around the world, there was always something powerful that happened when I knew I was in the presence of other believers. The Bible calls it a sweet fellowship of the saints. God strengthens us to live for Him oftentimes through others who also belong to Him. (Deuteronomy

33:3; Psalms 50:5; 145:9–10; Acts 2:41–42; and 2 Corinthians 8:4 are a few examples.)

As you persist in Bible study, prayer, and seeking the fellowship of believers, you'll find yourself growing. Christ will work in you and through you, and you will be able to say with Paul, "I can do all things through Christ who strengthens me" (Philippians 4:13). You will find miracles happening all around you as you discipline your life to the pattern of a true Christian.

Would you like to know that every sin is forgiven? Would you like to know that you are ready to meet God? It could happen today, if you will only let Christ come into your life. The Bible says that "whoever calls on the name of the LORD shall be saved" (Romans 10:13).

He extends an invitation to you. Will you open the door of your life to Him right now? You can do so by praying honestly and sincerely,

O God, I am a sinner. I repent of my sin. Forgive me and help me turn from my sin. I acknowledge what You have done on the cross for me and receive Your Son, Jesus Christ, as my Savior. I confess Him as my Lord. Give me faith to believe and trust as You lead me into obedience, relying on You in all things. Thank You for redeeming me and making me Your disciple. In Jesus' name. Amen.

No transcribed prayer grants a sinner salvation, but the Bible is clear that we must recognize our sin and repent of it, be willing for God to change us, and obediently follow Jesus Christ.

This is the most important step anyone can take in life and is the only way to truth. If you have entered into this new life, pray and ask the Lord to direct you to a Bible-believing, Bible-preaching church, where you can grow in the truth of God's Word and fellowship with His people. "And the Lord added to the church daily those who were being saved" (Acts 2:47).

Then please write to the following address so information can be sent to you to help you in your new journey with the resurrected Christ. God bless you.

—Billy Graham

Write to:
Billy Graham Evangelistic Association
1 Billy Graham Parkway
Charlotte, NC 28201

Notes

Introduction

1. Van Wishard, "Sleepwalking Through the Apocalypse," World Trends Research, http://www.worldtrendsresearch.com/articles /presentations/sleepwalking-through-apocalypse.html.

2. "World's Most Expensive Colored Diamonds" (slideshow), *Elle*, November 18, 2011, http://www.elle.com/accessories/bags-shoes -jewelry/worlds-most-expensive-colored-diamonds-610199 -10#slide-10.

3. The Hope Diamond, Harry Winston, http://www.harrywinston .com/our-story/hope-diamond.

4. Richard Rorty, *Philosophy and Social Hope* (London: Penguin Books, 1999), 204–8; http://www.answers.com/topic/hope#As _a_literary_concept.

5. Shawn Parr, "A Little More Hope Please," Fast Company, July 11, 2011, http://www.fastcompany.com/1766473/little-more-hope-please.

Chapter 1: Rescued for Something

1. Laura Hillenbrand, *Unbroken: A World War II Story of Survival, Resilience, and Redemption* (New York: Random House, 2010). See also Lev Grossman, "Top 10 Nonfiction Books," *Time*, December 9, 2010, www.time.com/time/specials/packages/article/0,28804 ,2035319_2034029_2034020,00.html.

2. John P. Coale's story is taken from an interview with Donna Lee Toney, transcript dated October 9, 2012, used by permission.

3. Descriptions of the night of the shipwreck compiled from several news sources, including those listed below, but especially Geraldo Rivera's special report, *Fox News Reporting: Tragedy at Sea,* broadcast January 22, 2012. See "Tonight—Tragedy at Sea: Geraldo Takes an In-Depth Look at the Italian Cruise Ship Crisis," *Fox News Insider,* January 22, 2012. Video clips from this special can be viewed on http://archive.org/details/FOXNEWS _20120129_060000_The_Five#.

4. "Costa Concordia Passenger: Titanic Theme Played As Ship Hit Rocks," *Huffington Post,* January 18, 2012, www.huffingtonpost .com/2012/01/18/titanic-theme-played-as-c_n_1213038.html.

5. Tom Kington, "Costa Concordia Purser: 'I Never Lost Hope of Being Saved,'" *The Guardian,* January 15, 2012, http://www .guardian.co.uk/world/2012/jan/15/costa-concordia-purser-saved.

6. Rivera, *Tragedy at Sea,* http://archive.org/details/FOXNEWS _20120129_060000_The_Five#start/989.5/end/1019.5.

7. Kathleen B. Carr, Elizabeth Duffy, David E. Sigmon, "A 'Small Technical Failure': Liability and Coverage Aspects Related to the Wreck of the Costa Concordia," *Claims Management: Strategies for Successful Resolution,* February 7, 2012, http://claims-management .theclm.org/home/article/Costa%20Concordia%20liability%20 insurance%20claims.

8. Stephen Cox, "The Titanic Effect," LewRockwell.com, January 20, 2012, lewrockwell.com/orig5/cox-s6.1.1.html; http://www .wariscrime.com/2012/01/20/news/the-titanic-effect.

9. Ibid.

10. "Divers Find 5 More Bodies in Costa Concordia Wreckage," CNN .com, March 23, 2012, http://www.cnn.com/2012/03/22/world /europe/italy-cruise-bodies/index.html. The total number of people on board was approximately 4,200, including a crew of 1,000.

11. "The Titanic in Documents and Photographs," *The Record: News from the National Archives and Records Administration,* March

1998, http://www.archives.gov/publications/record/1998/03/titanic.html.

12. Stephanie Pappas, "Costa Concordia vs. Titanic: Do They Compare?" LiveScience, January 18, 2012, http://www.livescience.com/18004-costa-concordia-titanic-comparison.html.

13. Rebecca Evans, Paul Harris, and Nick Pisa, "Captain Coward: 'I Only Left Because I Fell into Lifeboat When Ship Listed Suddenly as I Was Trying to Help,'" *Mail* Online, January 18, 2012, http://www.dailymail.co.uk/news/article-2087704/Costa-Concordia-Captain-Francesco-Schettino-I-left-I-FELL-lifeboat.html.

14. Diane LaPosta and Tim Lister, "Concordia Disaster Focuses Attention on How Cruise Industry Operates," CNN.com, July 4, 2012, http://www.cnn.com/2012/07/04/world/europe/costa-concordia. See also Pappas, "Costa Concordia vs. Titanic."

15. See Fiona Ehlers and Christian Wüst, "Doomed Cruise Ship Prepares for Final Voyage," *Spiegel* Online International, September 26, 2012, http://www.spiegel.de/international/europe/how-the-costa-concordia-will-be-salvaged-a-857683.html. According to this article, plans were being made in September 2012 to finally move the ship in May 2013.

16. Geraldo Rivera, *Tragedy at Sea*, author's transcript. Clips may be viewed at http://archive.org/details/FOXNEWS_20120129_060000_The_Five#start/300/end/330, http://archive.org/details/FOXNEWS_20120129_060000_The_Five#start/3389.5/end/3419.5, and http://archive.org/details/FOXNEWS_20120122_100000_The_Five#start/3420/end/3450.

17. See, for example, Evans, Harris, and Pisa, "Captain Coward" and Pappas, "Costa Concordia vs. Titanic: Do They Compare?"

18. Eve Conant, Barbie Latza Nadeau, "The Hidden Horrors of Cruise Ships," *The Daily Beast*, July 16, 2012, http://www.thedailybeast.com/newsweek/2012/07/15/concordia-aftermath-what-to-know-before-boarding-a-cruise-ship.html.

19. Kington, "Costa Concordia Purser," *The Guardian*, January 15, 2012.

20. Michael Inbar, "Rescuer: I Thought Man Beneath Burning Car Was Dead," *Today Heroes & Angels*, NBCNews.com, September 14, 2011, today.msnbc.msn.com/id/44499884/ns/today-good_news/t /rescuer-i-thought-man.

21. Michael Reagan, "Ronald Reagan at 100: The President, the Pope and the Medicine of Forgiveness," Opinion, Foxnews.com, February 6, 2011, www.foxnews.com/opinion/2011/02/06 /ronald-reagan-president-pope-medicine-forgiveness.

Chapter 2: The Great Redemption

1. Joseph Darnell, "Redemption: What Makes a Good Story Great—Movieology," podcast, *The American Vision*, May 24, 2011, http:// americanvision.org/4549/redemption-what-makes-a-good-story -great-movieology.

2. Roger Ebert, "In Search of Redemption," Roger Ebert's Journal, *Chicago Sun-Times*, June 27, 2008, http://blogs.suntimes.com /ebert/2008/06/in_search_of_redemption.html.

3. Bob Warja, "The 10 Best Redemption Stories in NFL History," *Bleacher Report*, December 22, 2011, http://bleacherreport.com /articles/989483-the-10-best-redemption-stories-in-nfl-history.

4. Daniel Terdiman, "Study: Americans Sitting on $30 billion in Unused Gift Cards," *CNET News*, January 24, 2011, http://news .cnet.com/8301-13772_3-20029410-52.html.

5. "Redeeming a Barnes & Noble Gift Card or eGift Card at Barnes & Noble.com," Barnes & Noble, http://barnesandnoble.com/gc /gc_redeem.asp.

6. R. Cody Phillips, *Operation Just Cause: The Incursion into Panama*, brochure (Fort McNair, DC: U.S. Army Center of Military History, n.d., ca. 1991), 3, http://www.history.army.mil /brochures/Just%20Cause/JustCause.pdf.

7. Timothy Lawn, "Operation Acid Gambit (1989)," Special Operations News, *Shadowspear Special Operations*, April 28, 2009,

http://www.shadowspear.com/special-operations/1458-operation
-acid-gambit.html.

8. William G. Boykin with Lynn Vincent, *Never Surrender: A
Soldier's Journey to the Crossroads of Faith and Freedom* (New York:
FaithWords, 2008), 187, 190.

9. Lawn, "Operation Acid Gambit (1989)."

10. Boykin, *Never Surrender*, 191.

11. Don Winner, "Army Honors Kurt Muse on 20th Anniversary of
Operation Just Cause in Panama," *Welcome to Panama Guide*,
December 26, 2009, www.panama-guide.com/article.php/army
-honors-kurt-muse.

12. Boykin, *Never Surrender*, 209.

13. Ibid.

Chapter 3: Sin Is In

1. Cathy Lynn Grossman, "Has the 'Notion of Sin' Been Lost?" *USA
Today*, February 22, 2012, http://www.usatoday.com/news/religion
/2008-03-19-sin_N.htm.

2. Ibid.

3. Ibid.

4. Ibid.

5. Ibid.

6. "15 Criminal Cases Solved with Digital Evidence," *Brainz:
Learn Something*, http://brainzorg/15-criminal-cases-solved
-digital-evidence.

7. Comments in response to a question by FlyboyOz on "Do You
Think That Sin Is Funny?" online forum at The Wings of the Web:
Airliners.net, May 14, 2003, http://www.airliners.net/aviation
-forums/non_aviation/read.main/391455, accessed August 24, 2012.

8. Paloma Espartero, "Spain," chapter 31 in *CEP: The European
Organisation for Probation* (uploaded PDF file), paragraph 4.4.2,
www.cepprobation.org/uploaded_files/Spain.pdf.

9. *Constitution of the Republic of South Africa, 1996*, section 84.2.j, http://www.info.gov.za/documents/constitution/1996/96cons5.htm#84.

10. *Wikipedia*, s.v. "Pardon," last modified December 20, 2012, http://en.wikipedia.org/wiki/Pardon.

11. "United States v. Wilson—32 U.S. 150 (1833)," Justia.com: US Supreme Court Center, 150–53, http://supreme.justia.com/cases/federal/us/32/150/case.html.

12. Ibid., 153.

13. Ethan Trex, "11 notable presidential pardons," January 5, 2009, CNN Living, http://articles.cnn.com/2009-01-05/living/mf.presidential.pardons_1_pardon-peter-yarrow-presidential-race?_s=PM:LIVING.

14. "United States v. Wilson—32 U.S. 150 (1833)," Justia.com: US Supreme Court Center, 160–61, http://supreme.justia.com/cases/federal/us/32/150/case.html.

15. Ibid., 161.

16. Ibid., 162.

17. "About E. Stanley Jones," E. Stanley Jones Foundation, http://www.estanleyjonesfoundation.com/about-esj/. Quotation from E. Stanley Jones, *Conversion* (New York: Abingdon, 1959), 69, in the Christian Quotation of the Day, June 7, 2005, http://www.cqod.com/index-06-07-98.html.

CHAPTER 4: THE PRICE OF VICTORY

1. Paul "Bear" Bryant, quoted in Pat Williams and Tommy Ford, *Bear Bryant on Leadership: Life Lessons from a Six-Time National Championship Coach* (Charleston, SC: Advantage, 2010), 147.

CHAPTER 5: WHERE IS JESUS?

1. Illustration taken from conversation between Kristy Villa and Donna Lee Toney, during taping of segment on the Billy Graham Library, September 16, 2011, Lifetime TV, *Balancing Act*, cohost Kristy Villa (stage name) for Olga Villaverde, aired October 21, 2011. Used with permission.

2. "The Virgin Birth of Jesus: Fact of Fable?" Religious Tolerance: Ontario Consultants on Religious Tolerance, www .religioustolerance.org/virgin_b.htm.

3. "Do Atheists Deny the Existence or Jesus, or His Resurrection?" comments by Eric_PK and Dave Hitt, Ask the Atheists, May 7–10, 2009, www.asktheatheists.com/questions/433-do-atheists-deny -the-existence-of-Jesus.

4. "Why Are Atheists More Skeptical About Jesus than They Are About Alexander the Great?" question posted on Ask the Atheists, October 25, 2007, www.asktheatheists.com/questions/114-why-are -atheists-more-skeptical-about-jesus.

5. Michael J. Cummings, "The Man of the Millennium," Cummings Study Guides, 2003, www.cummingsstudyguides.net/xbiography.html.

6. Ibid.

7. Derek Jacobi, quoted in Cummings, "Man of the Millennium."

8. Cummings, "Man of the Millennium."

9. "Shakespeare Facts: Read Facts About William Shakespeare," No Sweat Shakespeare, www.nosweatshakespeare.com/resources /shakespeare-facts.

10. Ben Jonson, "Preface to the First Folio (1623)," Shakespeare Online, http://www.shakespeare-online.com/biography/firstfolio .html, italics added.

11. Tom Reedy and David Kathman, "How We Know That Shakespeare Wrote Shakespeare: The Historical Facts," The Shakespeare Authorship Page, http://shakespeareauthorship.com /howdowe.html.

12. Ibid.

13. Cummings, "Man of the Millennium."

14. Ibid.

15. "Shakespeare Facts."

16. John Ankerberg and John Weldon, "The Evidence for the Resurrection of Jesus Christ" (PDF article), 5, Philosophy and Religion, www.philosophy-religion.org/faith/pdfs/resurrection.pdf.

17. *London Law Journal*, 1874, quoted in Irwin H. Linton, *A Lawyer Examines the Bible: A Defense of the Christian Faith* (San Diego: Creation Life Publishers, 1977), 36.

18. Ankerberg and Weldon, "Evidence for the Resurrection of Jesus," 6.

19. *Testimony of the Evangelists by Simon Greenleaf (1783–1853)*, http://law2.umkc.edu/faculty/projects/ftrials/jesus/greenleaf /html, Douglas O. Linder, "The Trial of Jesus: Online Texts & Links," Famous Trials, UMKC School of Law, University of Missouri-Kansas City.

20. William Lyon Phelps, *Human Nature and the Gospel* (1925), quoted in Howard A. Peth, *7 Mysteries Solved: 7 Issues That Touch the Heart of Mankind* (Fallbrook, CA: Hart Research Center), 206.

21. Charles Wesley, "Hymn for Easter Day" (1739), quoted in Collin Hansen, "Hymn for Easter Day," Christian History, http://www .christianitytoday.com/ch/news/2005/mar24.html.

22. Quoted in Ken Ham, "The Bible—'It's Not Historical,'" posted in AnswersinGenesis.org, April 1, 2003, www.answersingenesis.org /articles/au/bible-not-historical.

23. Josephus, *Jewish Antiquities*, 18.3.3, quoted in Gerald Sigal, "Did Flavius Josephus Provide Corroborative Evidence for Christian Claims?" Jews for Judaism, http://www.jewsforjudaism.org/index .php?option=com_content&view=article&id=158:did-flavius -josephus-provides-corroborative-evidence-for-christian-claims& catid=49:trinity&Itemid=501.

24. Tertullian, *Apology*, 5, quoted in Charles Germany, "The Historic Jesus," Rain of God, www.rainofgod.com/Article1.html, September 15, 2008, from T. D. Barnes, *Tertullian: A literary and historical study* (Oxford: 1971).

25. W. O. Clough, ed., *Gesta Pilati; or the Reports, Letters and Acts of Pontius Pilate, Procurator of Judea, with an Account of His Life and Death: Being a Translation and Compilation of All the Writings Ascribed to Him as Made to Tiberius Caesar, Emperor of Rome, Concerning the Life of Jesus, His Trial and Crucifixion*

(Indianapolis: Robert Douglass, 1880), http://books.google.com /books?id=IxY3AAAAMAAJ&pg=PA1&source=gbs_selected _pages&cad=3#v=onepage&q&f=false.

26. Julian the Apostate, quoted in Charles Germany, "The Historic Jesus," Rain of God, www.rainofgod.com/Article1.html, September 15, 2008, from *Against the Galileans*, (1923), 313–17.

27. Charles Germany, "The Historic Jesus," Rain of God, www .rainofgod.com/Article1.html, September 15, 2008. The phrase, "Vicisti, Galilaee," introduces Algernon Charles Swinburne's "Hymn to Proserpine" (1866), in which the poet imagines what Julian might have felt about the rise of Christianity. This poem may be found on The Victorian Web, http://www.victorianweb .org/authors/swinburne/hymn.html.

28. Plato, *Five Great Dialogues*, ed. and introduced by Louise Ropes Loomis, tr. B. Jowett (Princeton, NJ: Van Nostrand, 1942), 37, 38, 47. "I know that I know nothing," is the present-day recollection of the famous quote.

29. Louis Ropes Loomis, Introduction, in Plato, *Five Great Dialogues*, 7.

30. Creation Studies Institute, "Quotes About Jesus Christ," www .creationstudies.org/Education/quotes-about-jesus.html.

31. Augustine, quoted in J. Gilchrist Lawson, comp., *Greatest Thoughts About Jesus Christ* (New York: Richard R. Smith, 1930, orig. pub. 1919), 59.

32. Jean-Jacques Rousseau, *Profession of Faith of a Savoyard Vicar* (New York: Peter Eckler, 1889), 103–4.

33. Editors of baroquemusic.org, *Johann Sebastian Bach: His Life and Work*, PDF download (n.p.: New Horizon e-Publishers, n.d.), 25, http://www .newhorizonebooks.com/DLB05JohannSebastianBach.pdf.

34. Napoleon Bonaparte, quoted in John B. C. Abbott, "Napoleon Bonaparte, December 10, 1815," in *Harper's New Monthly Magazine*, 10 (December 1854–May 1855): 177–79.

35. Vincent Van Gogh, *The Complete Letters of Vincent Van Gogh: Volume III* (Boston: New York Graphic Society, 1978), 499.

36. Lord Byron, quoted in Herbert W. Morris, *Testimony of the Ages or Confirmation of the Scriptures* (Philadelphia: J. C. McCurdy, 1880), 737.

37. H. G. Wells, "The Three Greatest Men in History," *Reader's Digest*, May 1935, 12–13.

38. Charles Dickens, *The Letters of Charles Dickens*, ed. Graham Storey, vol. 12, 1868–1870 (New York: Oxford University Press, 2002), 12:188.

39. Daniel Webster, quoted in J. Gilchrist Lawson, comp., *Greatest Thoughts About Jesus Christ* (New York: Richard R. Smith, 1930, orig. pub. 1919), 133.

40. *Select Speeches of Daniel Webster, 1817–1845* (Boston: D. C. Heath, 1893), 391.

41. George Bancroft, quoted in J. Gilchrist Lawson, comp., *Greatest Thoughts About Jesus Christ* (New York: Richard R. Smith, 1930, orig. pub. 1919), 121.

42. Dr. Irmhild Baerend translated from original text. David Friederich Strauss, "Vergängliches und Bleibendes im Christenhum," 1838; also quoted in Philip Schaff, *The Person of Christ: The Miracle of History, with a Reply to Strauss and Renan and a Collection of Testimonies of Unbelievers* (Boston: The American Tract Society), 341.

43. Schaff, *The Person of Christ*, 48–49.

44. Ernest Renan, *The Life of Jesus* (New York: Random House/ Modern Library, 1955), 65, 393.

45. Sholem Asch, quoted in Ben Siegel, *The Controversial Sholem Asch: An Introduction to His Fiction* (Bowling Green, OH: Bowling Green University Popular Press, 1976), 148.

46. Sholem Asch, quoted in Frank S. Mead, ed. and comp., *The Encyclopedia of Religious Quotations* (Westwood, NJ: Fleming H. Revell Company, 1965), 49.

47. William Albright, *Archaeology and Religion of Israel* (Baltimore: Johns Hopkins Press, 1968, orig. pub. 1942), 176.

48. Nelson Glueck, *Rivers in the Desert: A History of the Negev* (New York: Grove Press, Inc., 1959), 31.

49. Kenneth Scott Latourette, *A History of Christianity,* vol. 1, *Beginnings to 1500,* rev. ed. (San Francisco: HarperSanFrancisco, 1975), 35, 44.

50. Mahatma Gandhi, *Gandhi on Non-Violence,* ed. Thomas Merton (New York: New Directions, 1965), 34.

51. Pinchas Lapide, *Jewish Monotheism and Christian Trinitarian Doctrine,* A Dialogue by Pinchas Lapide and Jürgen, trans. Leonard Swidler (Philadelphia: Fortress Press, 1981), 59.

52. Charles Malik, "These Things I Believe," http://www.orthodox .cn/catechesis/thesethingsibelieve_en.htm.

53. Malik, "Jesus Christ's Effect on Politics," Why-Jesus.com, http:// www.why-jesus.com/politics.htm.

54. Kenneth L. Woodward, "2000 Years of Jesus," *Newsweek,* March 28, 1999, 55, reprinted in *The Daily Beast,* http://www.thedailybeast .com/newsweek/1999/03/28/2000-years-of-jesus.html.

55. Charlton Heston, narrator, *Charlton Heston Presents the Bible: Jesus of Nazareth,* dir. Tony Westman (Burbank, CA: Warner Home Video, 2011), DVD. This quotation is also included in an editorial review on http://www.amazon.com/Charlton-Heston -Presents-Bible-Nazareth/dp/B004GSVX62.

56. Laura Alsop, "Decoding da Vinci: How a Lost Leonardo Was Found," CNN Living, November 7, 2011, http://www.cnn.com /2011/11/04/living/discovering-leonardo-salvator-mundi /index.html.

57. *Materializing Religion: Expression, Performance and Ritual,* eds. Elisabeth Arweck and William Keenan (Hampshire, England: Ashgate Publishing Limited, 2006), 166; Roy Greenhill, Sr., "Handel's *Messiah* Word Book, © 1998, http://tks.org/HANDEL /Messiah.htm.

58. Charlie, "Handel's Messiah: A Brief History," AnotherThink: One Christian's View of Post-Modern Life (blog), http://www .anotherthink.com/contents/movies_books_music/20051218 _handels_messiah_a_brief_history.html.

59. George Frideric Handel, "I Know That My Redeemer Liveth," http://www.tsrocks.com/h/handel_texts/aria_i_know_that_my _redeemer_liveth.html; to hear the music, look for one of the numerous performances on YouTube.

60. G. S. Viereck, "What Life Means to Einstein," *Saturday Evening Post*, October 26, 1929, 117. A transcript of this interview can be found online at http://www.einsteinandreligion.com /einsteinonjesus.html.

61. Pat Miller, "Death of a Genius," *Life*, May 2, 1955, 64.

62. Peter Larson, quoted in David C. McCasland, "God Intrudes," *Our Daily Bread*, December 12, 2006, http://odb.org/2006/12/12 /god-intrudes.

63. Unknown author, quoted in "Quotes about Jesus Christ," Creation Studies Institute, http://www.creationstudies.org/Education /quotes-about-jesus.html.

64. James Hastings, ed., *The Great Texts of the Bible: Genesis to Numbers* (New York: Charles Scribner's Sons, 1911), 407–8.

Chapter 6: Defining Christianity in a Designer World

1. Dave Thier, "Facebook Has a Billion Users and a Revenue Question," *Forbes*, October 4, 2012, http://www.forbes.com/sites /davidthier/2012/10/04/facebook-has-a-billion-users-and-a -revenue-question.

2. Jeremy Noonan, "The Quest for Belonging: The Social Network and 'The Inner Ring,'" Musing and Motion, March 1, 2011, http:// musingandmotion.wordpress.com/2011/03/01/the-quest-for -belonging-the-social-network.

3. Tim Ghianni, "Facebook 'Defriending' Led to Double Murder, Police Say," Reuters, February 10, 2012, http://in.reuters.com /article/2012/02/10/usa-facebook-murder-idINDEE81900L20120210.

4. Meghana RaoRane, "Where Do We Belong?" *Dancing with Happiness: Finding Your Bliss Everyday* (blog), November 22,

20011, http://www.dancingwithhappiness.com/2011/where
-do-we-belong.

5. Meghana RaoRane, "You Belong in YOUR Life," *Dancing with Happiness: Finding Your Bliss Everyday* (blog), September 8, 2011, http://www.dancingwithhappiness.com/2011/be-in -your-life.

6. Oliver Thomas, "Faith in America: Get Ready for Change," *USA Today* Forum, May 15, 2011, http://usatoday30.usatoday.com /news/opinion/forum/2011-05-15-The-future-of-religion_n.htm.

7. Austin Cline, "Designer Religion," Agnosticism/Atheism, About .com: Agnosticism/Atheism, August 15, 2003, http://atheism .about.com/b/2003/08/15/designer-religion.htm.

8. "'Designer' Ad Campaign for Church," *BBC News*, August 14, 2003, http://news.bbc.co.uk/2/hi/uk_news/3149919.stm.

9. Cathy Lynn Grossman, "More Americans Tailoring Religion to Fit Their Needs," *USA Today*, September 13, 2011, http://usatoday30 .usatoday.com/news/religion/story/2011-09-14/america-religious -denominations/50376288/1.

10. Ibid.

11. Ibid.

12. "God, religion, atheism; 'So What?'" *Asheville Citizen-Times*, January 8, 2012, reprint from Cathy Lynn Grossman; "For many, 'Losing My Religion' isn't just a song: It's life," *USA Today*, January 3, 2012, http://usatoday30.usatoday.com/news/religion/story/2011 -12-25/religion-god-atheism-so-what/52195274/1.

13. Grossman, "More Americans."

14. Ibid.

15. Robert Bellah, quoted in Grossman, "More Americans."

16. Ibid.

17. Grossman, "More Americans."

18. Quoted in Billy Graham, "University of Life," crusade sermon delivered November 15, 1980, Reno, Nevada.

19. Matt Buchanan, "Designing Windows 8 or: How to Redesign a Religion," Gizmodo, February 6, 2012, http://gizmodo.com /5882797/designing-windows-8-or-how-to-redesign-a-religion.

20. www.facebook.com/religionof.individualism.

21. Stephen Harvey, "How to Start a Religion," short film, *Current*, December 7, 2008, http://current.com/entertainment/comedy /89598648_how-to-start-a-religion.htm.

22. Michael Kress, "The 12 Most Powerful Christians in Hollywood" (slideshow), Kristin Chenoweth, Beliefnet, September 2008, http://www.beliefnet.com/Faiths/Christianity/2008/09/The-12 -Most-Powerful-Christians-in-Hollywood.aspx?b=1&p=9.

23. Description compiled from answers given to a question about the Coexist stickers in the Yahoo! Answers forum, http://answers.yahoo .com/question/index?qid=20100622155821AAID0JM. The bumper stickers reference a website called peacemaker.org and do not appear to be connected with the Coexist Foundation, whose website identifies it as "a charity established in 2006 to promote better understanding between Jews, Christians and Muslims—the Abrahamic Faiths— through education, dialogue and research." See http://www .coexistfoundation.net/en-gb/page/4/about-us.htm. The Coexist Foundation logo is superficially similar to the bumper stickers but contains only the symbols for Islam, Judaism, and Christianity.

24. The Chrislam.org website describes this organization as the Islamic-Christian National Dialogue Committee.

25. Meg Grant and Lawrence Grobel, "Sharon Stone Opens Up," AARP, January 19, 2012, http://www.aarp.org/entertainment /movies-for-grownups/info-01-2012/sharon-stone-interview.html.

26. Brett McCracken, "Hipster Faith," *Christianity Today*, September 3, 2010, http://www.christianitytoday.com/ct/2010/september/9.24.html.

27. Jon Meacham, "The Decline and Fall of Christian America," *Newsweek*, April 13, 2009, 36, reprinted as "The End of Christian America" in *The Daily Beast*, http://www.thedailybeast.com /newsweek/2009/04/03/the-end-of-christian-america.html.

28. http://www.imdb.com/title/tt0254007; *Wikipedia*, s.v. "Belonging," last modified December 20, 2012, http://en.wikipedia.org/wiki/Belonging_%28TV_series%29.

29. Alana Lee, "James Caan *Elf* Interview," BBC Home, November 2003, http:www.bbc.co.uk/films/2003/11/13/james_caan_elf_interview.shtml.

30. Starhawk, Wisdom Quotes: Quotations to Challenge and Inspire, http://www.wisdomquotes.com/quote/starhawk.html.

31. Craig Johnson, "Is Self-Marriage for You?" HLN, October 17, 2012, http://www.hlntv.com/article/2012/05/31/self-marriage-woman-marries-herself-would-you.

32. Katerina Nikolas, "Woman Marries Herself, Vows Lifelong Affair with Beautiful Self," *Digital Journal*, May 27, 2012, http://www.digitaljournal.com/article/325564.

33. Craig Johnson, "Is Self-Marriage for You?"

34. Zach Wahls, *My Two Moms: Lessons of Love, Strength, and What Makes a Family* (New York: Gotham, 2012).

35. See Jena McGregor, "Chick-fil-A President Dan Cathy Bites into Gay-Marriage Debate," Post Leadership (blog), *Washington Post*, July 19, 2012, http://www.washingtonpost.com/blogs/post-leadership/post/chick-fil-a-president-dan-cathy-bites-into-gay-marriage-debate/2012/07/19/gJQACrvzvW_blog.html.

36. Tony Patterson, "Dutch Heartbreak Hotel Gives 48-Hour Divorces," *The Independent*, http://www.independent.co.uk/news/world/europe/dutch-heartbreak-hotel-gives-48hour-divorces-2305618.html.

37. "The War on Baby Girls: Gendercide," *The Economist*, March 4, 2010, http://www.economist.com/node/15606229.

38. "MSNBC Host: 'Gendercide' Is a Constitutional Right," *The Blaze*, May 31, 2012, http://www.theblaze.com/stories/msnbc-gendercide-is-a-constitutional-right.

39. "About," Occupy Wall Street (website), http://occupywallst.org/about/.

40. "Hands Lyrics by Jewel," Songfacts Lyrics, http://lyrics.songfacts .com/detail.php?id=2350364.

41. Unnamed commenter on "Who Will Save Your Soul? by Jewel," Songfacts, http://www.songfacts.com/detail.php?id=1907.

42. "Who Will Save Your Soul? Lyrics by Jewel," Songfacts Lyrics, http:// www.azlyrics.com/lyrics/jewel/whowillsaveyoursoul.html.

43. Janice Taylor, "25 Ways to Feed Your Soul: Stop the Insanity," The Blog, *Huffpost Healthy Living*, May 18, 2012, http://www .huffingtonpost.com/janice-taylor/soul-tips_b_1512587.html.

44. Douglas Coupland, *The Gum Thief* (New York: Bloomsbury USA, 2007), 22.

45. Maria Theresa Ib, "Mind Over Myth?: The Divided Self in the Poetry of Sylvia Plath," www.sylviaplath.de/plath/dividedself.html.

46. "Edgar Allan Poe," Poet's Graves, http://www.poetsgraves.co.uk /poe.htm.

47. "12 Ways to Find Your SoulMate," Phyllis King: The Common Sense Psychic, http://www.phyllisking.net/submnu-12-Ways-to -Find-Ur-S.html.

48. The Puritan Board, "Great Reformed Quotes," Roderick E, February 11, 2009, www.puritanboard.com/f48/great-reformed -quotes-43723.

49. Simon Greenleaf, *The Testimony of the Evangelists: The Gospels Examined by the Rules of Evidence Administered in Courts of Justice* (Grand Rapids: Kregel Classics, 1995, orig. pub. 1874), 13.

50. Kyle Longest, "Finding Faith," *Furman: For Alumni and Friends of the University*, Spring 2012, 13.

51. Ibid.

Chapter 7: No Hope of Happy Hour in Hell

1. Michael Paulson, "What Lies Beneath: Why Fewer Americans Believe in Hell than in Heaven," Boston.com, June 29, 2008, http://www .boston.com/bostonglobe/ideas/articles/2008/06/29/what_lies _beneath/?page=full.

2. Publisher's note for Alice K. Turner, *The History of Hell* (New York:

Mariner Books, 1995), http://books.google.com/books/about
/The_history_of_hell.html?id=fFNkqzZ-U7MC., accessed April
23, 2013.

3. Jerry L. Walls, Books in Review, *The Formation of Hell* by Alan
   E. Bernstein (Ithaca, NY: Cornell University Press, 1994), http://
   www.leaderu.com/ftissues/ft9410/reviews/walls.html.

4. Jeff Long, "About the Author," RandomHouse.com, http://www
   .randomhouse.com/features/thedescent/author.html. The book
   discussed is Jeff Long, *The Descent* (New York: Crown, 1999).

5. *Tuscon Weekly*, editorial review of Cody Lundlin, *When All Hell
   Breaks Loose: Stuff You Need to Survive When Disaster Strikes*
   (Layton, Utah: Gibbs Smith, 2007), quoted on Amazon.com,
   http://www.amazon.com/When-Hell-Breaks-Loose-ebook/dp
   /B001OM52GK.

6. "Earth's Center Hotter than Sun's Surface," *The Birmingham
   News*, April 10, 1987, quoted in "Earth-Diameter," CBSENEXT,
   http://www.cbsenext.com/cfw/earth-diameter.

7. Dan Lathrop, quoted in Susan Kruglinski, "Journey to the Center of
   the Earth," *Discover*, June 8, 2007, 2, http://discovermagazine.com
   /2007/jun/journey-to-the-center-of-the-earth#.UO2ke3dGZOw.

8. Ibid.

9. "Derweze, Turkmenistan: The Gates of Hell," *Atlas Obscura*,
   http://atlasobscura.com/place/the-gates-of-hell.

10. Dante Alighieri, *The Inferno*, trans. Henry Wadsworth Longfellow
    (New York: Barnes & Noble Books, 2003, orig. pub. 1909), Canto
    III, line 9, page 14.

11. Stephen Greenblatt, "The Answer Man," *New Yorker*, August 8,
    2011, http://www.newyorker.com/reporting/2011/08/08/110808fa
    _fact_greenblatt?currentPage=all.

12. Ibid.

13. Ibid.

14. Ibid.

15. *Wikipedia*, s.v. "The Gates of Hell," last modified December 21, 2012,

http://en.wikipedia.org/wiki/The_Gates_of_Hell; for information about *The Thinker*, see http://www.musee-rodin.fr/en/collections /sculptures/thinker.

16. Lord De Cross, "Isaac Asimov—We Did Find the Genius Behind the Man," *Creative Writing for Entertainment*, http://lorddecross .hubpages.com/hub/Issac-Assimov-The-genius-behind-the-man.

17. "Isaac Asimov Top 10 Quotes," iPerceptive, www.iperceptive.com /topquotes/isaac_asimov_top_quotes.html.

18. Jean Rostand, "I should have no use for a paradise," Dictionary .com. *Columbia World of Quotations*, Columbia University Press, 1996. http://quotes.dictionary.com/I_should_have_no_use_for _a_paradise (accessed: January 09, 2013).

19. "Imagine Lyrics by John Lennon," Songfacts Lyrics, http://lyrics .songfacts.com/detail.php?id=773091.

20. "Wang Saen Suk Hell Gardens Welcome Visitors to Hell," TrendHunter Lifestyle, June 15, 2012, http://www.trendhunter .com/trends/wang-saen-suk-hell-gardens.

21. Michael Morris, Lynette Johns, Johan Scronen, Henri du Plessis, Norman Joseph, "When the Underworld Seeps into the Mainstream," iol News, August 4, 2003, http://www.iol.co.za/news/south-africa /when-the-underworld-seeps-into-the-mainstream-1.110849.

22. "Hell Ain't a Bad Place to Be—The Story of Bon Scott," PDF media release downloaded from bonscott.com, http://www .bonscott.com.au/bon/images/stories/the-story-of-bon-scott -media-release.pdf. See also the show's Ticketmaster page at http:// www.ticketmaster.com.au/Hell-Aint-A-Bad-Place-To-tickets /artist/1592642?tm_link-artist_artistvenue_module.

23. "Only the Good Die Young Lyrics by Billy Joel," Songfacts Lyrics, http://lyrics.songfacts.com/detail.php?id=180690.

24. Lyrics quoted in Dr. David R. Reagan, "Satan's Story: Past, Present and Future," Lamb & Lion Ministries, http://www.lamblion.com /articles/articles_doctrines8.php.

25. "Straight to Hell: Official Press Release," The Official Website:

KathyGriffin, November 5, 2007, http://kathygriffin.net/Press /nbc20071105.php.

26. Bandchris, comment on "Favorite Kathy Quotes," Kathy Griffin Official Forum, October 14, 2008, http://kathygriffin.net /phpBB2/viewtopic.php?f=5&t=15685&start=30.

27. George Bernard Shaw, *Man and Superman* (1903), act 3, Bartleby .com, http://www.bartleby.com/157/3.html.

28. Alan Cairns, "Alan Cairns > Quotes," GoodReads, http://www .goodreads.com/author/quotes/140391.Alan_Cairns.

29. Home page, *The Gates of Hell* website, www.thegatesofhellmovie.com.

30. *Neighbors from Hell*, TBS.com, About the Show, http://www.tbs .com/stories/story/0,,218318,00.html.

31. Ben Marshall, "What is Hell.com and how do I get in?" TV and Radio Bog, *The Guardian*, 18 July 2007, www.guardian.co.uk /culture/tvandradioblog/2007/jul/18/whatishellcomandhowdoig.

32. Stephen (last name kept private), "What Is / Was Hell.com— The Real Answer," The Coffee Desk, October 27, 2009, http: //thecoffeedesk.com/news/index.php/2009/10/27/what-is -www-hell-com.

33. "Overview" (of topic of Hell in videogames), Giant Bomb, http:// www.giantbomb.com/hell/95-24.

34. "Hell Divine Releases 'Upcoming Hell Volume VI' Anthology," Metal Underground, March 17, 2012, www.metalunderground .com/news/details.cfm?newsid=78561.

35. "Metallica—The Prince Lyrics," Lyrics007, http://www.lyrics007 .com/Metallica Lyrics/The Prince Lyrics.html.

36. "AC DC—Highway to Hell Lyrics," Lyrics007, http://www .lyrics007.com/AC DCLyrics/Highway To Hell Lyrics.html.

37. "Venom—Satanachist Lyrics," Lyricsty, http://www.lyricsty.com /venom-satanachist-lyrics.html.

38. Justin Donnelly, interview with Geezer Butler, reposted as "Heaven and Hell's Geezer Butler Discusses 'The Devil You Know,'" Blabbermouth.net, April 20, 2009,

http://www.blabbermouth.net/news.aspx?mode=Article&newsite mID=118460.

39. "Humanists of the Year," American Humanist Association, www .americanhumanist.org/AHA/Humanists_of_the_Year.

40. Judi McLeod, "Ted Turner May Have Inspired UN 13 Moon Calendar," *Canada Free Press*, May 19, 2005, http://www .canadafreepress.com/2005/cover051905.htm.

41. Ted Turner, speaker for National Press Club Luncheon, September 27, 1994, transcript (Washington, DC: Federal News Service, Inc., 1994), 23.

42. Cliff Vaughn, "Ted Turner Talks About His Faith," Ethics Daily, February 28, 2003, www.ethicsdaily.com/ted-turner-talks-about -his-faith-cms-2247.

43. Norman Mailer, *On God: An Uncommon Conversation* (New York: Random House, 2007), 21.

CHAPTER 8: HE IS COMING BACK

1. Robbie Collin, "The Dark Knight Rises: A Comprehensive Review," *The Telegraph*, July 19, 2012, http://www.telegraph.co.uk /culture/film/filmreviews/9412391/The-Dark-Knight-Rises-a -comprehensive-review.html.

2. Geoff Boucher, "'Dark Knight Rises': Christopher Nolan's Gotham, Back in Black," Hero Complex (blog), *Los Angeles Times*, July 21, 2012, http://herocomplex.latimes.com/2012/07/21/dark -knight-rises-christopher-nolans-gotham-back-in-black.

3. Ernstthomas18 (reader/reviewer), "Absolute Perfection," Reviews and Ratings for The Dark Knight Rises, IMDb, 7 July 2012, http:// uk.imdb.com/title/tt1345836/reviews?start=20.

4. Dave Trumbore, "New Look at THE DARK KNIGHT RISES Batsuit; Christopher Nolan Comments on his BATMAN Trilogy," Collider.com, January 11, 2012, http://collider.com/Christopher -nolan-the-dark-knight-rises-batsuit/137256.

5. Quoted in Boucher, "Dark Knight Rises."

6. Quotes from *The Dark Knight Rises*, www.imdb.com/title
/tt1345836/quotes; and "A Fire Will Rise" promotional trailer for
the film, https://buz.fm/buz.php/25222618/Premiering-July-20th
-A-Fire-Will-Rise-and-The-Legend-Will-End---The-Dark-Knight
-Rises.

7. Chelsea J. Carter, "Movie Massacre: 'Oh My God, This Is Really
Happening,'" CNN.com July 27, 2012, http://www.cnn.com
/2012/07/20/us/colorado-shooting-narrative/index.html; www.cnn
.com/2012/07/20/us/colorado-theater-suspect-profile/index.html.

8. Ibid.

9. Comments from survivors heard in television news reports at the
scene of the shooting that night.

10. Bryan Enk, "Christopher Nolan Calls Colorado Shooting
'Unbearably Savage,'" July 20, 2012, http://www.nextmovie.com
/blog/christopher-nolan-colorado-official-statement.

11. Jeff Jensen, "Batman. Bane. Catwoman. That Ending! Time to
Talk About 'The Dark Knight Rises'—But Only if You've Seen It,"
EW.com PopWatch, July 21, 2012, http://popwatch.ew.com
/2012/07/21/batman-bane-catwoman-that-ending-time-to-talk
-about-the-dark-knight-rises-but-only-if-youve-seen-it.

12. John W. Gardner, *No Easy Victories*, ed. Helen Rowan (New York:
Harper Colophon, 1968), 57.

13. Quoted in BJ Penner, "BJ Penner: A Different World" (letter to the
editor), *Merced Sun-Star*, http://www.mercedsunstar.com/2012
/01/11/2187711/bj-penner-a-different-world.html.

14. Admiral Jim Stockdale, quoted in Jim Collins, *Good to Great: Why
Some Companies Make the Leap . . . and Others Don't* (New York:
Harper Business, 2001), 85.

15. Quoted in Billy Graham, "University of Life," crusade sermon
delivered November 15, 1980, Reno, Nevada.

16. "That's My King," (transcript and video clips), Not Just Notes!
http://www.notjustnotes.ws/thatsmyking.htm; YouTube; Dr. S. M.
Lockridge, "Do You Know Him? That's My King."

17. "Doomsday Clock ticks one minute closer to Armageddon," *The Telegraph*, January 10, 2012, http://www.telegraph.co.uk/news /newsvideo/9006352/Doomsday-Clock-ticks-one-minute-closer -to-to-Armageddon.html.
18. Paul Alster, "Taking the Pulse of Armageddon as Israel-Iran Showdown Looms," FoxNews.com, August 25, 2012, http://www .foxnews.com/world/2012/08/25/taking-pulse-armageddon-as -israel-iran-showdown-looms/#ixzz2BmzrLR48.

ABOUT THE AUTHOR

BILLY GRAHAM, WORLD-RENOWNED AUTHOR, PREACHER, and evangelist, has delivered the Gospel message to more people face-to-face than anyone in history and has ministered on every continent of the world in more than 185 countries. Millions have read his inspirational classics, including *Angels, Peace with God, The Holy Spirit, Hope for the Troubled Heart, How to Be Born Again, The Journey,* and *Nearing Home.*